INSIGHT COMPACT GUIDES

ST. PETERSBURG

Compact Guide: St Petersburg is a culture-based guide for a culture-based destination, revealing the splendours of the city's monuments, the wealth of its museums and the delights of its streets, squares and canals.

This is one of almost 100 titles in Insight Guides' series of pocket-sized, easy-to-use guidebooks intended for the independent-minded traveller. Compact Guides are in essence travel encyclopedias in miniature, designed to be comprehensive yet portable, as well as up-to-date and authoritative.

Star Attractions

A instant reference
to some of
St Petersburg's
most popular tourist
attractions to help
you on your way.

*Peter and Paul
Fortress p14*

Palace Square p28

Russian Museum p35

*Nevsky Prospekt – a
shopping arcade p37*

Rossi Street p38

Summer Garden p42

Smolny Cathedral p47

Mariinsky Theatre p53

*Hermitage
Museum p70*

Grand Palace at Peterhof p74

ST. PETERSBURG

St Petersburg – the Venice of the North

The second largest city in Russia and one of the world's major cities, St Petersburg has played a vital role in both Russian and European history. For two centuries it was the capital of the Russian Empire. Founded as St Petersburg (Russian: Sankt Peterburg) by Peter the Great in 1703, it was renamed Petrograd in 1914 and Leningrad in 1924. The name St Petersburg was restored in 1991.

Statue of Peter the Great

St Petersburg was not only the stronghold of the tsars, but also of revolutionaries, and the city is renowned as the scene of the February and October revolutions of 1917. It is also renowned for the role it played in World War II, when for 872 days the local populace fiercely defended their city against the remorseless German siege.

In the decades following the war, St Petersburg was restored to its former glory. Although, today, many of its buildings and monuments are once again in a dilapidated state of repair, it is the architectural charm of the city, its elegance and harmony, which continues to make it so popular with visitors. The pleasingly symmetrical streets and squares, quiet canals and uniquely styled bridges provide a vivid contrast to the more untamed beauty of the surrounding countryside. Officially proclaimed the 'cultural capital of Russia', St Petersburg has a rich and varied cultural palette, offering much more than simply the Hermitage Museum and the Kirov Ballet of the Mariinsky Theatre. In St Petersburg there is more in the way of theatre, concerts, opera and rock and roll than any other city in the country.

St Petersburg is also associated with many of the past greats of Russian culture. Among those who have lived and worked here on their immortal creations are poets and writers such as Pushkin, Dostoyevsky and Gogol, the Realist painter Repin, the composers Tchaikovsky and Glinka as well as the architect Rastrelli. Stage artists such as Kommissarzhevskaya, Chaliapin and Pavlova have performed in the city's theatres.

In St Petersburg, where the first Russian Science Academy was founded on the orders of Peter the Great, there are now over 300,000 students, studying at 47 universities and 92 technical colleges. There are over 70 museums, 2,600 libraries and 300 scientific research institutes.

It would be naive to assume that it is possible to obtain a complete picture of Russia by means of one or even several trips. Consequently, it is necessary to select from the rich geography of this country. However, no visit to Russia which excludes a tour of St Petersburg can hope to provide an adequate picture of the history and culture of this country, of its customs and traditions, its greatness and its beauty.

5

Opposite: Double-headed eagle on the Church of the Resurrection

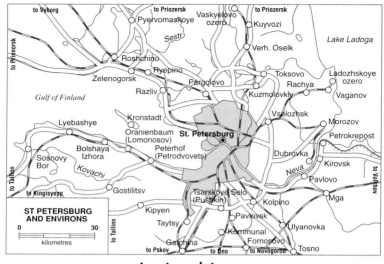

Location and size

The city is located on the delta of the Neva River at the head of the Gulf of Finland, at 60°N and 30°E, on the same latitude as southern Alaska, the southernmost point of Greenland, and Oslo. St Petersburg spreads across some 44 islands of the delta and across neighbouring parts of the floodplain. The city has always been prone to flooding because of its flat and low-lying terrain, but this has been alleviated by the construction of a dyke across the Gulf of Finland. No fewer than 60 rivers and streams as well as canals with a total length of over 160km (100 miles) pass through the city and surrounding area. These make St Petersburg a city of waterways and bridges and have earned it the nickname 'Venice of the North'.

Flowing out of Lake Ladoga to the east, the Neva itself is only 74km (46 miles) long. Within St Petersburg, this river and its various tributaries divide the central part of the city into four distinct sections. The Admiralty Side, where much of the city's historical and cultural heritage is concentrated, runs along the left (south) bank of the Neva. Between the two major arms of the Neva, the Bolshaya (Great) and Malaya (Little) Neva, is Vasilievsky Island. The Malaya Neva and its tributary known as the Bolshaya Nevka enclose a group of islands known as the Petrograd Side; the Vyborg Side constitutes part of the mainland to the east.

The city covers an area of 606 sq km (234 sq miles), although Greater St Petersburg, forming a horseshoe shape around the Gulf of Finland and encompassing such historic towns as Oranienbaum and Peterhof in the west, as well as Zelenogorsk on the north shore, is much larger.

A cruise boat on the Neva river

Climate

St Petersburg has a moderate, maritime climate, which is the mildest on this latitude in Russia. The warmest month is July (average temperature: 18°C/64°F), the coldest January (average temperature: −8°C/18°F). There are on average 222 days per year with a temperature recording over 0°C (32°F), of which 126 are with rainfall.

Generally there is snow from the beginning of November to the middle of April, though there are winters without much snow.

Summertime on the beach near the Peter and Paul Fortress

The weather in St Petersburg is never particularly stable: the temperature can fluctuate up to 6°C (43°F) between the different areas of the town. The Gulf of Finland's bathing season lasts from the middle of June until the end of August; the water temperature during this time ranges from 14–24°C (57–75°F).

In summer the White Nights (where day does not become night) are most apparent from the beginning of June to early July. During this time the city has a very particular magic. The steeples of the cathedrals, the tips of the city towers, and the stained-glass windows of the palaces and churches shine in what seems to be an unending twilight; even at night, downtown St Petersburg is full of people.

From November to the end of March the Neva and its canals are mostly frozen.

Industry

St Petersburg has long enjoyed international acclaim for its industries, which include shipbuilding and machinery construction, electrical engineering, chemicals, textiles, leather, fur and food industries, the construction of large electric turbines and the production of electronic, optical and other precision apparatus. The St Petersburg seaport is the country's largest and, even though the Baltic freezes over during the winter, icebreakers keep the port open all year round.

Bust of Engels in the garden of the Smolny Institute

Politics and economy

Together with the Ukraine and Belorussia, Russia represents the historic core of the once-great Russian Empire which ended with the October Revolution in 1917. Even after the disintegration of the Soviet Union in 1991, the country remains by far the largest of the former Soviet Socialist Republics.

As a result of the democratisation that followed Mikhail Gorbachev's *Perestroika* (restructuring), begun in 1986, as well as the failed coup of conservative politicians in August 1991, an almost 75-year-old Communist dictatorship came to an end as did its corresponding Soviet state system. Since then there have been enormous changes.

A one-party state has been transformed into a fledgling multi-party democracy, and a socialist-planned economy – and all the stability that went with it – has had to give way to the forces of the free market.

The workings of the free market have had a huge effect on all Russians. The immediate effects of the freeing of prices in 1992 were a plummeting rouble and rampant inflation – and the recent crash in the rouble has seen the return of rocketing prices. Although Western consumer goods are now widely available they are unaffordable for most Russians whose wages – particularly in the state sector – have barely risen. The changes have also led to a dramatic reduction in industrial output and economic freedom unaccompanied by the mechanics of regulation has resulted in the emergence of organised crime on an unprecedented scale.

Despite this, many co-operative and small private companies have been established, shops and restaurants have proliferated and within the framework of joint-venture agreements old Soviet and foreign firms have merged to work with one another. There is now an emerging mon-eyed middle class – the so called 'novo-russkiye' or new Russians – although that term also carries with it gangsterish overtones. But it is this new class that appears to be most threatened by the recent economic crisis.

Buying records and compact disks in Melodiya

People

St Petersburg is the most northerly city in the world with more than 1 million inhabitants. Today, more than 5 million people live here, not only Russians, who make up the vast majority of the population, but also Ukrainians, Belorussians and representatives from many other nations of Russia and the former Soviet Republics. Prior to the Revolution, the city had sizable Baltic, Polish and German as well as smaller Tatar, Chinese and Jewish communities. Between the wars the city continued to act as a magnet for peasant labour, and even after World War II the newcomers tended to outnumber the locals. Be that as it may, the people of St Petersburg have many common traits, including their sophistication. The atmosphere of old St Petersburg may be long gone, but in this city designed as a cultural centre, many of the citizens consider themselves to be the most cultivated of Russians. In keeping with the city's traditional role as Russia's window to the world, the inhabitants maintain a cosmopolitan outlook, open to deal with the vast changes coming their way.

The people of St Petersburg have always shown great resilience in the face of adversity. Beggars and child labour – nothing new in Russia's turbulent history – may be back on the streets, but there remains nevertheless an overriding feeling of optimism.

Musicians in period costume

Historical Highlights

More than a thousand years ago the region now encompassing St Petersburg and the surrounding areas was inhabited by Slav tribes, who in the 10th century joined the association of the Kievan Russians, an early feudal state created in eastern Europe at the turn of the 9th century. The Slavs' main trade route ran this way, through the Gulf of Finland, along the Neva and across Lake Ladoga (from the Varangians – Vikings – to the Greeks); it connected north and south Russia, the Baltics and Scandinavia with Byzantium.

12th century This region became part of the Novgorod feudal republic. Its favourable geographical position and the attempt to cut the Russians off from the sea attracts special attention from the neighbours in the north.

13th–14th century The Swedish kings try on numerous occasions to annex these countries, but without success.

1617 The Swedish army manages to occupy the banks of the Neva and to set up the Nyenschanz Fortress at the mouth of the Oka River which flows into the Neva. As a result Russia is cut off from the Baltic.

1700 The beginning of the Great Northern War between Russia and Sweden. Russia attempts to regain access to the Baltic.

1702 The Swedish Noteborg Fortress at the source of the Neva is recaptured. The fortress was actually set up by the Novgorods and later occupied by the Swedes. Peter I describes it as a key castle, ie key to the future city of St Petersburg.

1703 At the beginning of May the Nyenschanz Fortress also falls at the hands of the Russian troops. On 16 May (27 May according to the Gregorian calendar) Peter I commands the Saint Peter Fortress to be built on the small Hare Island (Zayachi Ostrov) on the widest section of the Neva estuary where the river divides into two streams – the Great and Little Neva. From the fortress (later renamed the Peter and Paul Fortress) it is possible to observe every enemy approach from either the Great or Little Neva. St Petersburg is founded at the same time as the fortress and with its position on the banks of the Baltic is expected to become the 'window to Europe'. A year is needed before the first city streets are built under the cannon's protective shield.

Factories and various manufacturers begin to rise from the marshes and the forest. Printing companies establish themselves successfully in the town, the first newspapers and magazines appear, the maritime academy is opened (1715), followed soon after by artillery, engineering and medical schools, the first museum (1719) and later the science academy (1725).

1721 Russia wins the final victory in the Great Northern War. Peter I (the Great) adopts the title of tsar and is consequently the country's leading spiritual and secular power.

1724 Peter I has the top state institutions moved from Moscow to the banks of the Neva. The Guards regiment establish their garrison here. St Petersburg becomes the official capital of Russia. Soon most court-related families move there.

First priority is given to the establishment of brickworks, shipbuilding industries, and a military base. Next comes the stock exchange and the commercial centre with its appropriately named streets such as Liteiny (founder), Kanatny (ropemaker), Smolyanoy (pitch burner) and the Monetny (coin) yard. The gunpowder factory, sugar factory, brewery, porcelain factory and the cotton, calico and textile manufacturing industries are all established in the city.

1725 Peter I dies on 25 January. His heirs Catherine I, Peter II and Anna Ivanovna devote far less energy on the state, but spare no expense in having their residences luxuriously furnished. It is Peter's daughter Elisabeth, reigning from 1741–61 and Catherine II (the Great) – born Princess von Anhalt-Zerbst, reigning from 1763–96 – who continue with Peter's plan. His dream was that the new Russian capital's royal suburb of Petrodvorets should excel the beauty of Versailles in France. Like Peter, they summon the best Russian and foreign architects to St Petersburg, many of whom make Russia their second home.

1812 The Russian army defeats Napoleon's Grande Armée. This event is soon overtaken by the creation of magnificent architectural memorials in St Petersburg.

1824 The biggest flood in the history of the city does tremendous damage to many buildings, parks and gardens. At the beginning of the 19th century the secret Northern Company is set up. The goal of its members is to put an end to the autocracy of the tsar and the yoke of serfdom. They are the first generation of Russian revolutionaries.

The exceptional luxury in which the aristocracy lives is in stark contrast to the unbelievable poverty of the working population. The growing anti-feudal movement among the farmers arouses the forward-thinking intellectuals of the time, whose views had been developed under the influence of the Enlightenment and the French Revolution.

1825 On 14 December – during the interregnum due to the sudden death of Alexander I – revolutionary-minded young aristocratic officers and the 3,000 soldiers and sailors under their command try to fire a revolt with a view to forcing the tsar Nikolai (Nicholas) I into abdicating his rights to the throne. This rebellion, known as the Decembrists' Uprising, is cruelly suppressed. Five of the leaders are executed, and more than 500 officers sentenced to forced labour and prison.

In the following years a second wave of the freedom movement develops in St Petersburg.

1835 Opening of the first Russian railway, linking St Petersburg with Tsarskoye Selo (the tsar's village, formerly Pushkin).

1851 Opening of the regular train connection between St Petersburg and Moscow.

1861 Official abolition of serfdom. Tsars Nicholas I, Alexander III and Nicholas II invest all their ambitions in having the Orthodox Byzantine kingdom re-established. Chernyshevsky and then Plekhanov, influenced by Marxist theories, create the foundations for a new world. Public opinion is roused by means of leaflets, magazines from the underground movement, declarations by writers and journalists, paintings by a group of touring artists called the Peredvizhniki (Wanderers) and the martyrs of the revolutionary cause. There are an increasing number of assassinations. The prisons are full and there are numerous deportations.

1879 In St Petersburg the revolutionary organisation Narodnaya Volya (People's Will) is founded, which organises the assassination of Tsar Alexander II on 1 March 1881.

1890 Lenin's first trip to St Petersburg. As an external student he completes his legal studies at the university.

1893 From now on the scattered anarchist and revolutionary powers begin to form a single, large movement under the leadership of Lenin and his party. For Lenin, the revolution could almost be said to be a private family matter: an older brother was executed in the Peter and Paul Fortress because of his involvement in an assassination attempt on Alexander III, his other brothers were, with the approval of their mother, glowing fighters for the revolutionary cause. During periods of exile in Siberia or abroad, Lenin with the help of like-minded friends transforms Marxist theories to Russian reality, dedicating himself to the political education of the workers in the factories, built both south of the Narva Triumphal Arch and in the northern quarter of the city.

1895 Lenin sets up the Union for the Struggle for the Liberation of the Working Class in St Petersburg. From this organisation the proletarian revolutionary party emerges.

1903 The Russian Social Democratic Labour Party splits into two factions: Bolsheviks (majority) and Mensheviks (minority).

1905 A strike breaks out in the Putilov Works and is supported by other industries in the city. On Sunday 9 January about 140,000 St Petersburg workers march to the Winter Palace bearing a petition to the tsar. They are met by troops who open fire; more than 100 marchers are killed and hundreds more wounded. History records this day as Bloody Sunday. The incident causes a general revolt, joined by some sections of the army and navy. The tsar is obliged to make a few concessions which are, however, withdrawn soon afterwards. Among these concessions is the establishment of the Duma, or State Assembly, which is provided with very limited rights.

The period from 1905–7 is recorded in Russian history as the first bourgeois revolution.

1914 At the beginning of World War I against Germany, the German name of the city (St Petersburg) is changed to the Russian name of Petrograd.

1917 World War I brings Russia to the brink of economic and political catastrophe. During the

February Revolution, Tsar Nicholas II abdicates his rights to the throne. In Petrograd the Provisional Government is set up with the Socialist Revolutionary lawyer Kerensky at its head. He calls for the continuation of war against Germany. Until this point it has been a bourgeois revolution. In April 1917 Lenin returns from exile in Switzerland to change this middle-class revolt into a proletarian revolution. However, after his defeat in July, he is pursued by the Provisional Government, and goes into hiding. On 10 October the Bolshevik Central Committee under Lenin's leadership (Trotzky and Stalin are also members) decide on an armed revolt. On 25 October (7 November in the Gregorian calendar) they gain control of the insurgent Petrograd. History records this day as the day of victory for the 'Great Socialist Revolution'.

After seizure of power, the Soviet government under the leadership of Lenin's Bolsheviks and Socialist Revolutionaries, nationalises industries and introduces agricultural reforms, as well as negotiates peace treaties.

1918 On 3 March the Brest-Litovsk peace treaty is signed. On 12 March the government leaves Petrograd and moves back to Moscow. After Lenin's death (1924) Petrograd becomes Leningrad.

1941–4 In June the German troops outflank the Red Army and begin to encircle Leningrad. On 8 September rail links to the city are cut off and the Blokada (siege) – which is to last for 872 days – begins. Soon, the city's almost 3 million inhabitants have to contend with no heating, no water supply, almost no electricity and very little food. But they do not surrender. The treasures of the Hermitage and the suburban palaces are hidden. Dmitri Shostakovich writes his Leningrad Symphony, which is performed in the besieged city. Several hundred thousand people are evacuated from Leningrad across Lake Ladoga via the famous 'Road of Life' – the only route connecting the city with the mainland.

Today, there are few signs left of the siege or the damage it caused. A foreigner, even a young person from St Petersburg, would hardly be able to believe the tragic truth of that winter of 1941–2 when temperatures reached –35°C (–31°F), and 650,000 people starved and froze to death.

1944 After the full lifting of the siege on January 27, the people of St Petersburg set about rebuilding their city.

1950 The production levels of the city reach the level they were at before the war. In Primorsky Pobedy Victory Park the Kirov Stadium is built.

1955 The first underground station is opened.

1965 On 8 May, exactly 20 years after the 'Great War for The Fatherland', Leningrad is given the honorary title of 'City of Valour'.

1986 The beginning of the reorganisation of the country's entire political and social lifestyle is initiated by Mikhail Gorbachev. His new policies of *Perestroika* (restructuring) and *Glasnost* (openness) are soon internationally recognised terms.

1990 The law which guarantees the leading role of the Communist Party is abolished at the III Congress of the party representatives in Moscow, and the creation of other parties is authorised.

1991 In June Boris Yeltsin, having resigned from the Communist Party, becomes the first democratically elected president of Russia. In August an attempted coup by communist hardliners is suppressed without bloodshed in the then Leningrad. After a city-wide referendum, St Petersburg is readopted as the name of the city. The Presidents of Russia, Belarus and the Ukraine sign a treaty to abolish the USSR and form the Commonwealth of Independent States (CIS). On 25th December Gorbachev resigns and the USSR ceases to exist.

1993 After parliamentary opposition to his programme of privatisation Yeltsin holds and wins a nationwide referendum in support of reforms.

1996 Yeltsin narrowly defeats the Communist Party leader Gennady Zyuganov in the July presidential elections despite growing concern about his health after two serious heart attacks. In December, after two years of fighting, Russian troops begin to withdraw from the breakaway republic of Chechnya.

1998 In July the bodies of Nicholas II and his family are buried in the Cathedral of St Petersburg's Peter and Paul Fortress. In August, after three years of relative economic stability, the rouble crashes leading to galloping inflation. In response to the crisis Yeltsin is forced to accept Yevgeny Primakov as his new prime minister after parliament rejects his preferred candidate Victor Chernomyrdin.

Route 1

Detail of the Troitsky Bridge

Peter-and-Paul Fortress – Petrograd Side – Vasilievsky Island

The Petrograd Side (Petrogradskaya Storona) of St Petersburg encompasses the islands of Hare, Petrograd, Apothecary and Peter. It was on Zayatschy Ostrov (Hare Island) that Peter the Great is said to have laid the foundation stone for the ★★★ **Peter and Paul Fortress** ❶ (Petropavlovskaya Krepost, Wednesday to Monday 11am–6pm, in winter 11am–5pm, closed Tuesday).

From the city centre, now located on the left bank of the Neva, take the underground to Gorkovskaya station. Another good alternative is to walk across the Troitsky Bridge, from where there are beautiful views across the river to the Palace Embankment and to Vasilievsky Island in the west.

History

14

Prison room in the Peter and Paul Fortress

Built to protect Russia, the fortress did not actually see active combat until 25 October 1917. For more than 200 years the cannons did not fire a single shot. However, not even 10 years had gone by before the fortress had been transformed into a dreaded prison. One of the first political prisoners was Peter I's son; Tsarevich Aleksei was suspected of participating in a conspiracy against his father. He died under torture in 1718.

The first Russian aristocratic revolutionary, the writer Alexander Radischev, author of *A Journey from St Petersburg to Moscow*, awaited his execution here in 1790. The death sentence was lifted at the last moment and Catherine II gave orders that the prisoner was to serve 10 years in Siberian exile.

The leaders of the Decembrists' Revolt, Bestushev-Rumin, Pestel and Rileyev, were imprisoned in the Secret

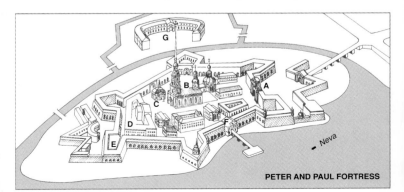

PETER AND PAUL FORTRESS

House of the Alekseyev trench, the prison for hardened criminals. The novelist Dostoyevsky, the revolutionary democrat, philosopher, critic and writer Chernyshevky and the writer Pisarev also served sentences here. The vast majority of the convicted revolutionaries of the 1880s sat in the cells of the Trubetskoy Bastion, among others the members of the Narodnaya Volya Party. It was in the casemate of this fortress that the last meeting between Lenin's mother and his elder brother took place. Lenin's brother was executed 10 days later for his participation in the assassination attempt on Tsar Alexander III. At the beginning of the 1920s Lenin's companions Bauman and Lepechinksky were imprisoned in solitary confinement. In January 1905 Gorky was brought to this prison. Suffering from tuberculosis, it was here that he wrote his play *Child of the Sun*. The Trubetskoy Bastion has been preserved exactly as it was in 1872. In 1922 the fortress became a museum.

Sightseeing

Turn left after the Troitsky Bridge and cross another small bridge (Ioann Bridge) to reach the St John's Gate (Ioannovskiye Vorota) and **Peter's Gate** [A] (Petrovskiye Vorota) leading into the fortress. This triumphal arch was built according to plans by Trezzini in 1718. Statues of Bellona (god of war) and Minerva (goddess of wisdom, the arts and crafts) were placed in the niches of the gate to symbolise the wisdom of Peter I.

Peter's Gate

15

From Peter's Gate a straight alley leads to what is, from an art historian's point of view, the most valuable monument in the fortress, the ★★ **Peter and Paul Cathedral** (Petropavlovsky Sobor) [B], which was built between 1712–32, also according to the plans of Trezzini. The centrepiece of the fortress, the cathedral is considered to be a good example of 18th-century Russian architecture, modelled on the Dutch and German styles. The interior is 61m (200ft) long and 16m (52ft) high; the bell tower is 122m (402ft) high. The carved, gold iconostasis is one of the most superb examples of Russian wood-carving in existence. Taking five years to complete, the iconostasis was modelled from sketches drawn up by Zarudny.

Interior of the Peter and Paul Cathedral

The cathedral crypt contains the white-marble tombs of the Russian tsars with the exception of Peter II and Ivan VI. In July 1998 the burial took place for the bodies of the executed Nicholas II and his family. Even today, fresh flowers are regularly placed on the tomb of Peter I. The imperial eagle, in gilded bronze, decorates only the Romanov tombs, the rulers of Russia for 300 years. To the right of the southern entrance it would be impossible to miss the two enormous tombs made of Altai jasper and Urals rhodonite. They are the those of Tsar Alexander II

The Boat House

and his wife, the Hessian princess Maria Alexandrovna. Every 15 minutes the old Dutch clock (restored in 1987) chimes from the belltower built between 1762–6.

Next to the cathedral stands a beautiful columned pavilion, crowned by a sculpture of the sea goddess. This is the **Boat House** [C] (Botniy Dom), which once housed the small English boat that Peter the Great learned to sail in on the River Jausa. Peter I's boat is described as the 'Grandfather of the Russian fleet'. Today it can be seen in the Central Naval Museum on Vasilievsky Island.

In the west wing of the fortress is the **Mint** [D] (Monetniy Dvor), the city's oldest business, installed in the fortress on Peter I's command in 1724. The present buildings were built between 1798–1806 by Antonio Porto. In the days of the tsar, gold, silver and copper coins were minted here; today, coins, medals and medallions are made here, as were the pennants carried by Russian spaceships to the Moon, Mars and Venus.

Behind the Mint is the **Trubetskoy Bastion** [E], mentioned on page 15. Leading out to the Captain's harbour the **Neva Gate** [F] (Nevskiye Vorota), in the south of the fortress, has a very colourful past. It was also called Death Gate, because prisoners sentenced to death were – if not executed there and then – led through this gate to the boat which was to take them to their place of execution. Every day at noon a cannon is fired here, which nowadays marks the beginning of the lunch break.

The Neva Gate

The cannon were not always used for such peaceful purposes. In October 1917 the garrison soldiers joined with the insurgents. On 25 October (7 November), the headquarters ordered that the Winter Palace be stormed after the cannon shot was fired from the *Aurora* cruiser during the night of 25 October (7 November). It was under the covering fire of the Peter and Paul Fortress that the

Provisional Government was toppled. For the first time in 214 years, the fortress took part in active combat.

There are two other permanent exhibitions within the grounds of the Peter and Paul Fortress: **Petrograd's History from 1703–1917** and **The Architecture of St Petersburg-Petrograd**. To the left of the Ioann Bridge, when leaving the Peter and Paul Fortress, an obelisk is visible on the other side of the canal. It was here that the ill-fated Decembrists were executed (*see Historical Highlights*). During the hanging the rope broke three times, with the result that one of the three prisoners concerned broke a leg. However, as opposed to revoking the death penalty, as was customary under such circumstances, the men were hanged a second time.

Old cannons at the Artillery Museum

Within the grounds of the crown-works in the outworks of the fortress is the Gothic-styled red building of the former arsenal, which now houses the ★ **Artillery, Engineering and Communication Forces Museum** [G] (Wednesday to Sunday 11am–5pm). Founded by Peter the Great in 1703, the weapon collection currently contains approximately 70,000 exhibits. It ranges from 15th-century swords to 20th-century ballistic missiles.

17

To the east of the Peter and Paul Fortress, on the Petrograd side, is **Troitskaya Ploschad ❷**. On the left side of the square (Kronverksky Prospekt 1/2) is the villa of the former prima ballerina, Mathilde Kschessinska. In March 1917 the house was used as the Bolshevik Party headquarters and Lenin addressed the crowds from the balcony. Built by Gogen in 1905, and a good example of the Style Moderne, it now houses the **Museum of Russia's Political History ❸** (formerly the October Revolution Museum), where various changing exhibitions are held.

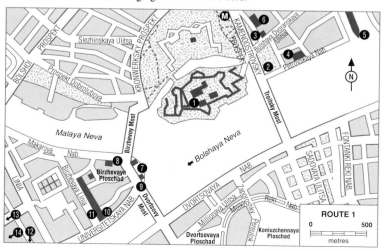

There is also a permanent display about the ballerina herself, as well as a new wax exhibition on the gruesome death of Tsar Nicholas II and his family (daily 11am–5pm except Thursday, Wednesday 11am–4pm).

Interior of Peter the Great's Cottage

To the southeast of Troitskaya Ploschad (Petrovskaya Naberezhnaya 6) is **Peter the Great's Cottage ❹** (Domik Petra Velikogo, Wednesday to Monday 10am–5.30pm, closed Tuesday). This was the city's first domestic residence; it was built by soldiers in a few days in May 1703. From here Peter the Great could comfortably observe the construction of the capital's fortress and other buildings. The captain and crew of the first foreign ship to bring wares to St Petersburg gave the tsar (who piloted the sloop that came out to meet them) 5,000 gold roubles. This Dutch ship was renamed *Petersburg* and continued to sail the same route for another 50 years.

The Aurora cruiser

Following the road east along the river, the road bends towards the quay, where the legendary ★ *Aurora* **cruiser ❺** (Kreyser Avrora) is anchored. Launched in 1903, the ship is now a branch of the Central Naval Museum (10.30am–4pm, closed Monday and Friday).

On 27 May 1905 the cruiser took part in the battle against the Japanese at Tsushima Bay, during which the Russian fleet was defeated. In February 1917 the crew of the cruiser hoisted the ship's red flag for the first time. From then on the *Aurora* was an important mobile support of the Bolsheviks in their fight against the Kerensky government. During the night of 25 October, the cruiser sailed into the Neva and trained its guns on the Winter Palace, residence of the Provisional Government. At 9.45pm the forward gun of the *Aurora* fired a blank shot, giving the signal for the Winter Palace to be stormed. The victorious leader of the revolution, Lenin, immediately transmitted a declaration to the citizens of the revolution over the ship radio, informing them of the proceedings. After World War I the *Aurora* became a training ship. During World War II the guns were used once again, this time against the German enemy laying siege to the town.

On the other side of the Great Neva on the Pirogovskaya Embankment is a modern building housing the St Petersburg Hotel.

The Great Mosque

Back in Troitskaya Ploschad in the north one can see the two slim minarets and blue-tiled dome of the **Great Mosque ❻** (Metchet), the only mosque in St Petersburg. It was built in 1912 by S Kritschinskiy and Vasilyev using funds provided by the Islamic community and was modelled on the Gur-Emir Shrine in Samarkand. There were many Moslem tatars and kalmucks living in the town even during Peter the Great's reign. They were regarded as being among his most trusted servants. The interior of the building is decorated in accordance with Islamic tradition: the columns are layered in green marble, Quranic verses are engraved on the enormous chandeliers in the middle of the room. The building is presently closed for renovation, although prayers are still held.

The Kamenoostrovsky Prospekt curves round the Lenin Park in a wide semicircle, inside which is the ★ Zoo and the planetarium. The Prospekt ends near Builders' Bridge (Most Stroitelei), which links the Petrograd side with Vasilievsky Island. Turning off right shortly before the bridge is Prospekt Dobrolyubova and the modern buildings of the Yubileyny sports complex.

Located on the tip of Vasilievsky Island are what are considered to be the finest examples of architecture in St Petersburg. This island, opposite the Admiralty and the Angliskaya (English) Embankment and encircled by the Great and Little Neva as well as the Smolyenka River, is the largest island in the Neva Delta. The spit, Strelka, its easternmost point, juts out into the river where the Great Neva divides with the Little Neva (magnificent view).

Birzhevaya Ploschad – one of the Rostral Columns

19

The Strelka is taken up by ★ **Birzhevaya Ploschad** ❼ (Stock Exchange Square). On the slope down to the Neva on both sides of the large semi-circular square in front of the Stock Exchange are the two Doric-styled **Rostral Columns** (1810, by von de Thomon). These 32-m (105-ft) columns were originally built as signal towers and navigational flares were burnt on the capitals. They lit the way for the ships to the Neva moorings. Later the fires were replaced by gas lights, still lit today on national holidays. In accordance with ancient Roman tradition, the columns were decorated with ships' prows, which for the sake of the symbolism were sawn off from captured enemy vessels. At the foot of the columns colossal figures represent Russia's great trade rivers – the Volga, Dnieper, Volkhov and Neva.

The Strelka used to be the main city harbour. After the main harbour was moved to the west bank of Vasilievsky Island at the beginning of the 19th century, the old harbour buildings were put to other uses. The former Customs House (by Luchini and Stasov, 1832), built in the style of late Russian Classicism, now houses the **Russian Literature Institute of the Academy of Sciences** ❽ (Institut Russkoi Literatury – Pushkinsky Dom, Monday to Friday 10am–6pm, closed Saturday and Sunday). The palatial rooms of the Institute (4 Naberezhnaya Makarova), commonly called Pushkin House, contain a variety of archival material such as letters and samples of handwriting of almost all the most significant Russian authors of the 18th and 19th century. The exhibition at the museum shows the development of Russian literature from the first edition of the ancient Russian epic *The Song of Igor's Campaign* up to the present day.

Russian Literature Institute of the Academy of Sciences

Model Ships in the Central Naval Museum

The **Central Naval Museum** ❾ (Voyeno Morskoi Muzei, Wednesday to Sunday 10.30am–5pm), is housed in the former stock exchange (1804–11, by Thomas de Thomon). The building is a copy of the Greek temple of Paestum. It is surrounded by a peristyle with 44 Doric columns; the enormous staircase leads to the main floor (stocks and bonds) of the former stock exchange. Since 1940 it has contained the Central Naval Museum. The foundation for the collection was provided by Peter the Great, who started collecting ship models in 1709. Among the 500,000 exhibits are 1,500 models of ships that served in the Russian fleet. As mentioned earlier, the museum also contains Peter I's boat (*see page 16*).

West of the Strelka, stretching along the south of Vasilievsky Island between the Palace Bridge and the Nikolayevsky Bridge, is the University Embankment (Universitetskaya Naberezhnaya). The warehouses at No 1 have been turned into the **Zoological Museum of the Academy of Sciences** ❿ (daily except Friday 11am–5pm). The academy, in its role as an institute, used to house the following museums and collections: the zoological museum, the academy library, the anthropological and ethnological museum as well as the Lomonosov museum. One highlight of the Zoological Museum is a mammoth, which lived over 44,000 years ago. It was found in the permafrost of Yakntsia, Siberia, in 1901.

The Siberian mammoth

Worth particular attention is the former Kunstkamera, which was founded by Peter I and now contains the **Museum of Anthropology and Ethnography**, and a museum dedicated to Lomonosov, the learned chemist, physicist, geologist and grammarian (1711–65). Before Lomonosov worked in these rooms, they were used to house the exhibits of the first natural science museum, commissioned by Peter I. Visitors came to admire the astonomical instruments, maps, rare books, minerals and other things collected in part by the tsars themselves. In order to encourage visits from citizens who did not yet know what a museum was, there was no charge and foreign visitors received a glass of vodka at the entrance. Among the exhibits in the **Lomonosov Museum** is the so-called Gottorp Globe, which is over 3m (10ft) wide.

The Gottorp Globe

When at the end of the 18th century the former academy building had been outgrown by its exhibits, a new academy building, the Academy of Sciences (5 Glavnoye Zdaniye Akademy), designed by Quarenghi, was built in Classical style next door (1788). It is very different from the Kunstkamera and the adjoining buildings which are in the characteristic baroque style of the early 18th century. Stretching along the Neva, the main facade of this three-storey building is adorned with a monumental portal consisting of eight Ionic columns. Inside, the palatial staircase

Peter's Room in St Petersburg University

and white conference room, with its 18th- and 19th-century furnishings, are both well worth seeing. Next to the academy building is a bronze memorial to Lomonosov (by Sveschikov and Petrov).

The former seat of the 12 ministries of state (*kollegi*) is now **St Petersburg University** ⓫ (St Petersburgsky Gosudarstvenny Universitet). Around 20,000 students are currently studying at its 15 faculties. Designed by Trezzini, the building was constructed between 1722–41 as a complex with 12 identically large buildings. Not originally intended as a university, the building was the seat of the 12 *kollegi*, (ministries furnished according to the needs of Peter the Great). In 1830 the buildings were affiliated to the university, founded by Alexander I a few years earlier (1819). Inside, only Peter's Room has been preserved in its original form, though it is not open to the public.

On the embankment are three other buildings dating from the 18th century which have belonged to the university at various points. The first house (No 11) is Tsar Peter II's former palace; the second (No 13) was used as headquarters for the first officer cadets; and the yellow building (No 15) which has the date 1710 written on the gable is the **Menshikov Palace**, an ornately styled baroque building. The tsar was accustomed to receiving foreign ambassadors here. This palace was one of St Petersburg's first stone houses. Having made a gift of the house and the entire island to his closest advisor Menshikov in 1701, Peter the Great took it back in 1714. Today its exhibits reflect Russian culture during the reign of Peter I (Tuesday to Sunday 10am–4.30pm, closed Monday).

Behind the Rumyantsev garden, in which there is a black granite obelisk commemorating the victory of the Russian army over the Turks, led by Field Marshal Rumyantsev (1768–74), is the ★ **Academy of Fine Arts** ⓬ (Akademiya Khudoshestv, Wednesday to Sunday

21

Bust of Peter in the University

The Academy of Fine Arts

11am–7pm). Built by Kokorinov and De la Motte between 1764–88, the edifice is considered to be one of the finest examples of 18th-century Russian architecture. It stands out both because of the originality of its location and the artistic wealth of its interior. Many important Russian painters and sculptors attended this academy which was founded in 1757, and many of their works are on display.

Housed in the academy is the St Petersburg Institute for Painting, Plastics and Architecture and there is also a museum in memory of the famous Ukranian artist and poet Shevchenko, who lived and worked here from 1826–34.

In front of the main facade of the Academy of Arts is a quay, constructed in strict Classical style (1834, by Thon). The granite used for the statues of the sphinxes and griffins came from Thebes, the old Egyptian capital. For this reason the mooring is also called Sphinx Quay.

Sculpture on the Sphinx Quay

The University Embankment runs into the Niko-layevsky Naberezhnaya. Looking down the road to the right – 8 Linia – it is be impossible to miss the **Church of the Annuciation** (Blagovechtchenskaya Tserkov, 1765) on the corner Maly Prospekt. It is a good example of how old Russian building components were used in 18th-century architecture in St Petersburg.

Statue of Admiral Kruzenstern

The streets running north to south on Vasilievsky Island are named as and numbered by *liniya* or lines. On the embankment – between the 11 and 13 Linia – is a residence, formerly belonging to Field Marshal Münnich and later reconstructed by Volkhov in 1796, the **Naval Cadet Corps** ⑬ (Morskoi Kadetskoy Korpus). In front of the academy on the quay there is a statue of Admiral Kruzenstern, under whose command Russian ships sailed round the world at the beginning of the 19th century. Kruzenstern died in 1846.

A bit farther on (corner of Embankment/15 Linia) is a church that belonged to the town house maintained in St Petersburg by the Kiev Cloister (Kiev Petscherskaya Lavvra). It is now used once again as a place of worship.

Coal and Steel Institute

At the end of the quay is the **Coal and Steel Institute** ⑭ (Gorny Institute; 1806–8; architect: Voronichin) with an imposing Doric colonnade.

The massive walls of the building and the two groups of sculptures by Demut-Malinovsky (left: *Attack on Proserpina*, right: *Hercules Fights with Antaeus*) were created to portray man's bond with the earth, and consequently emphasise the purpose of the building. The Coal and Steel Institute contains extensive information about mining technology and the coal and steel industry (entrance: 21 Linia, house No 2).

North of the embankment, stretching from east to west, almost parallel, are the Bolshoi (Great), Sredny (Middle) and Maly (Small) Prospekts/Avenues of Vasilievsky

Island, all laid out in the 18th century. Many houses have been retained from that period including the Lutheran **Church of St Catherine** (Bolshoi Prospekt 1, by Velten) with a four-columned portal with bas-reliefs and sculptures in the niches.

In 1937, the monumental **Kirov Palace of Culture** (Dvorets Kultury im Kirova) was built on the Bolshoi Prospekt, with a theatre able to seat 1,300 people, a dance room for 1,500 people, a restaurant and over 100 club rooms. The architects were Totsky and Kazakov and the building is an impressive example of 1930s architecture.

In the southwestern section of the island, the Bolshoi Prospekt ends at Ploschad Morkoy Slavy (Square of Maritime Glory) where the **St Petersburg Port and Sea Terminal** (St Petersburgsky Morskoy Vokzal) is located. Almost all passenger ships arrive at this terminal with the exception of large vessels with too great a draught. On the right side of the square are two identical small towers. These are the lookout posts that were used at the time of the tsars. From the top of these so-called crown heads, cannons guard the entrance to the harbour, once the mooring of the galley fleet.

St Petersburg Port and Sea Terminal

Nearby is the **Pribaltiskaya Hotel** and the exhibition halls, where international fairs are held. From Ploschad Morskoy Slavy, to the left if your back is facing the River Neva, it is possible to see the **port** where foreign freight and passenger ships drop anchor. The Neva is over 1km (½ mile) across here at the mouth of the Gulf of Finland.

The new western section of Vasilievsky Island, bordered by the Gulf of Finland, and the northern Decembrists' Island (Ostrov Dekabristov) is the closest new residential area there is to the old centre. Over the past few years a modern estate has been built here.

Ships on the River Neva

Wedding in front of the Monument of Peter the Great

Route 2

Senate's Square – St Isaac's Square – Palace Square

The Commission for the Development of St Petersburg put forward the idea of building three parade grounds in the city centre in the middle of the 18th century. However, 100 years passed before the ensemble of Senate's Square, St Isaac's Square and Palace Square had been completed.

★★ *Senate's Square*

Senatskaya Ploschad (Senate's Square) was renamed Decembrists' Square in 1925 in commemoration of the Decembrists' revolt on 14 December 1825. Now reverted to its original name, the attractive square has a broad view of the River Neva.

In the middle of the square is the famous ★★ **Monument of Peter the Great** ⓰ (Medny Vsadnik), known as *The Bronze Horseman*. On an enormous granite base (1,600 tons) shaped like the crest of a wave, Peter I rides a rearing horse. Commissioned by Catherine the Great and designed by Etienne Maurice Falconet, this monument is regarded as one of the most important examples of 18th-century sculpture. It dominates the entire square and underlines the significant role of Peter I in Russian history and the development of the city.

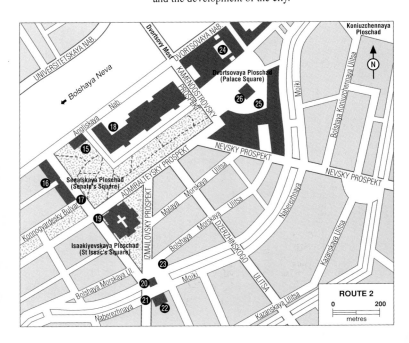

To the west, the square is bordered by two cream-coloured buildings, richly decorated with columns and figures. They are linked by an arch which stretches across Galernaya Ulitsa. Within are the old **City Archives** ⓰. During the days of imperial Russia this was the head-quarters of the Senate and the Holy Synod, the highest secular and spiritual institutions after the monarchy. Constructed by Rossi in neoclassical style, they represent his last major work (1834).

Adjoining this building in the north is the neoclassical **Riding School of the Cavalry Guard** ⓱ (Konnog-vardeyski Manesh). The building resembles an ancient Greek temple. It was built according to Quarenghi's designs in 1807. The middle section of the columned hall is decorated with a double colonnade and statues of the Dioscuri, sons of Zeus. The statues were prepared in Italy and modelled on the Quirinale Palace in Rome (1817, Triscorni). This building, which served for only a short time as a riding school, was later used for exhibitions. Johann Strauss gave concerts here. Today it is the Association of Fine Arts' exhibition hall.

The east side of the square is occupied by the cream-coloured ★★ **Admiralty** ⓲ (Admiralteystvo). It was built

Detail on the Admiralty facade

between 1806–23 by Zacharov on the site once monopolised by the shipyards responsible for launching the first Russian ships during Peter the Great's reign. The Admiralty has always been regarded as one of the most beautiful buildings in the city. Now it is also listed in the UNESCO directory of world heritage sites. The significance of the building as a symbol of the seafaring strength of the country is impressively emphasised by its sculptures. Over the middle section, the gilded tip of the spire is crowned by a weather vane in the form of a golden sailing ship (total height 72.5m/238ft), the emblem of St Petersburg. Today, the building is regarded as the architectural centrepiece of St Petersburg.

The side of the Admiralty bordering Senate's Square measures 163m (535ft), and the facade which stretches from Admiralty Prospekt on Senate's Square to Palace Square is 407m (1335ft) long. Bordered to the south by the Neva, there is a superb view from Senate's Square across the river to the right bank and the Peter and Paul Fortress, the Rostral Columns and the University Embankment. From the harbour, the riverboats offer a number of interesting excursions along the Neva.

Between Senate's Square and St Isaac's Square stands St Isaac's Cathedral which is well worth seeing.

★★ St Isaac's Square

★★ **St Isaac's Cathedral** ⓳ (Isaakiyevsky Sobor; Thursday to Tuesday 11am–7pm, last admission 6pm; Colon-

St Isaac's Cathedral

Bronze bas-relief on the front entrance of St Isaac's Cathedral

Statue of Nicholas I

nade observation point Thursday to Tuesday 11am–6pm, last admission 5pm; closed Wednesday) took almost 40 years to construct. It was designed by the French architect Montferrand (1819–58) and work was overseen by Stasov and the Michailov brothers. The cathedral with its huge dome is 105.5m high (346ft) 111.2m long (365ft) and 97.6m wide (320ft). It can accommodate 14,000 people.

The building is decorated with 112 red granite columns, as well as bronze statues and domes which are covered in over 100kg (220lbs) of pure gold. The exterior of the 5m- (16ft-) thick walls is clad in grey marble and inside, in addition to the 14 varieties of marble, many different kinds of natural stones were used, with the result that the cathedral practically doubles as a museum of minerals.

The front entrance is decorated with bronze bas-reliefs depicting biblical themes. On the west side in the lower left-hand corner is a semi-reposed figure of a man in a toga. It portrays Montferrand holding a model of St Isaac's Cathedral. The interior furnishings of the cathedral – pictures, frescoes, mosaics, windows and in particular the painting on the ceiling of the main dome by Brullov – are all as breathtaking as each other. The state did not spare any expense decorating the most important cathedral of the capital: the total costs incurred were almost 10 times those incurred for the tsar's residence and the Winter Palace.

In 1931 the cathedral was turned into a museum. Until 1988 the largest Foucault pendulum in the world (weight: 54kg/119lbs, length 93m/305ft) was one of the many pieces on exhibit; however, it was not hung up again after its renovation. This pendulum can be used to show the rotation of the earth.

A visit to the Colonnade observation point at the base of the dome (300 steps) affords a magnificent view of the city.

To the west of the cathedral is another building that was also constructed using drawings by Monferrand and whose facade partly mirrors the facade of the cathedral. To the south on the corner of the Pochantskaya Ulitsa is the square's oldest building, definitely significant from an artistic point of view. It is the **Mayatlev Palace**, thought to have been built by Rinaldi in 1760. The French Encyclopaedist Diderot lived here from 1773–4. Pushkin, a friend of the poet Mayatlev, was also a regular guest.

In the southern section of the square is the **Statue of Nicholas I** [20]. The equestrian statue, designed by Peter von Klodt-Jürgensburg, was cast in 1859.

The Moika River cuts through St Isaac's Square and is spanned by the **Blue Bridge** [21] (Siniy Most), which is about 90m (300ft) wide and 35m (115ft) long. Until serfdom was abolished in Russia in 1861, the bridge, which was painted blue at that time, was the arena for a sort of slave market, ie the buying and selling of serfs. Just over the bridge is the **Town Hall** ㉒ the former Mariinsky Palace (Mariinsky Dvorets). It was built by Stakenschneider for Maria, the oldest daughter of Nicholas I. Today the palace houses the St Petersburg City Council. The Intourist Office is now located in house No 11, built originally as the German Embassy before World War I by Behrens. On the west side of the square is the Institute for the Protection of Plants, the famous Vavilov Institute, and on the east side the Botanical Institute.

The Town Hall

Further up the Moika at No 94 is the **Yusupov Palace**, built by De la Motte in the 1760s. This is where Rasputin was murdered by Felix Yusupov in 1918. English-language tours are available by prior arrangement (tel. 314-9883). Russian-language tours for individual tourists start at 11.10 am, 12.10 pm, 1.10 pm, 2.10 pm, 3.10 pm.

On the corner of the Bolshaya Morskaya Ulitsa is the **Astoria Hotel** ㉓. With its splendid interiors, the hotel is a fine example of the successful architectural experiments performed in the early 20th century (1912, by Lidval). It is known that the leaders of the German Army had planned to hold a reception in the banqueting hall of the Astoria upon capturing the city and had even printed invitations which were found in Berlin after the War among the remains of the Third Reich's headquarters.

The lobby of the Astoria Hotel

Bolshaya Morskaya Ulitsa runs across both sides of St Isaac's Square. On its southwest side are three noteworthy houses: At No 52 is Polovtsev's House (1835 by Pel) which houses St Petersburg's Architects' Association, and has a beautiful restaurant. Opposite, at No 45, is Princess Gagarina's House (1845 by Montferrand), today the Composers' House (Dom Kompositorov). Next door, No 47 is where the famous emigré writer Vladimir Nabokov, author of *Lolita*, was born.

From the Astoria Hotel, Bolshaya Morskaya Ulitsa runs northeast. Together with the parallel-running **Malaya Morskaya Ulitsa**, this was once the main thoroughfare of the St Petersburg metropolis. Large banks, credit and insurance companies were based here, an example being the Russian Bank of Trade and Industry (Bolshaya Morskaya Ulitsa 15). Peretyakovich designed this house in 1910 to match the spirit of Russian Classicism using motifs from the Italian Renaissance.

Many of Russia's outstanding intellectuals and wealthy town dwellers have lived in Malaya Morskaya Ulitsa. Nikolai Gogol lived at No 17 from 1833–6; here he wrote *Dead Souls* and *The Inspector General*. Piotr Tchaikovsky lived and died at No 13. Fiodor Dostoyevsky lived from 1847–9 at No 23 and Alexander Herzen lived at No 25.

From 1832–3 Alexander Pushkin lived in No 26, where he worked on his novel *Dubrovsky*. The most famous Russian jewellers, Fabergé, had their shop at No 24.

★★★ *Palace Square*

After passing the crossroad (Bolshaya Morskaya Ulitsa with Nevsky Prospekt) and two magnificent triumphal arches (*see page 30*) you reach ★★★ **Palace Square** (Dvortsovaya Ploschad). Although the surrounding buildings reflect very different period styles, the overall effect is of a harmonious whole.

Soldiers in Palace Square

Many events that have had an important effect on the course of Russian history have taken place in this square. It provided the stage for the events that shook the Russian imperium, brought down the imperial throne and heralded the foundation of the Soviet Union.

On 9 January 1905, the day referred to as Bloody Sunday in the history books, 140,000 demonstrators, mainly workers with members of their families, marched to the Winter Palace with icons, flags and pictures in order to hand a petition to Nicholas II. They were led by Father Gapon, who it was later said was a police spy. The army was waiting for them and opened fire. More than a hundred people were left dying in the snow and many more were wounded. This was the beginning of the 1905 revolution that Lenin described as the dress rehearsal for the October Revolution.

It was in this square that in February 1917 the tsar's standard was lowered from the flagpole, never to be raised again, and later on 25 October (7 November) that sections of the Red Guard as well as soldiers and sailors sympathetic to the cause stormed the former imperial palace, in which the middle-class Provisional Government, surrounded by what was left of its loyal troops (including a female batallion), was hiding. The revolutionaries' attack

The old General Staff Building in Palace Square

on the Winter Palace on 7 November (25 October according to the Julian calendar) and the capture of members of Kerensky's Provisional Government (Kerensky escaped to the USA) marked the beginning of the 1917 Revolution.

The entire north side of the square is taken up by the main (south) facade of the ★★★ **Winter Palace** ❷ (Zimny Dvorets), residence of the Russian tsars from Peter's daughter Elisabeth to the end of the Romanov dynasty. The palace, for over 200 years the focus of attention for the entire Russian population, is the most magnificent of the Russian palaces. It is the work of the famous Italian architect Bartolomeo Rastrelli (1700–71). When Rastrelli's father, the sculptor Carlo Rastrelli, who lived in Paris, was invited by Peter the Great to come to Russia, son followed father and Bartomeo subsequently pursued most of his career in St Petersburg.

The Winter Palace

Work began in 1754, on the request of Elisabeth Petrovna, Peter the Great's daughter, who reigned for 20 years (1741–61). Since the Empress and the architect both shared the same preference for the powerful, slightly Italianate Russian baroque, the palace was generously provided with stucco, statues, columned halls and colonnades. Even at the time it was in a baroque world of its own (1,050 rooms, 1,787 windows, 117 staircases), although it was still not complete by the time Elisabeth Petrovna died. Peter III, who only reigned for a few months, was not interested in continuing the work. He was followed by Catherine II who was more interested in Classicism, perhaps because Classicism had just come back into fashion in Paris. She had the work finished and also had the Small Hermitage added by Vallin de la Motte.

29

Statues on the Winter Palace

Only the brick facade and the ground floor survived the fire that gutted the palace in 1837; however, just 18 months later Vasily Stasov and Aleksandr Brullov had finished the restoration. On its completion an extravagant gala was held to receive the foreign ambassadors. Although Rastrelli put his distinctive mark on the Winter Palace, the arrangement of the rooms still corresponded to the taste of that period.

The Winter Palace is lavishly decorated with marble, malachite, jasper, bronze, fine wood, rock crystal and precious stones. The Hermitage Museum opened in 1946 and incorporates many palaces, of which the Winter Palace is the largest. The other palaces are: the Small Hermitage (1764–5, by Vallin de la Motte), the Old Hermitage (1771–87, by Velten), the Hermitage Theatre (1783–7 by Quarenghi) and the New Hermitage (1839–52, by von Klenze and Stakenschneider). These five buildings as well as their famous collections are described in a separate section (*see The Hermitage Museum*).

The Small Hermitage

The former Guard Corps Headquarters

Tourists and touts

Bust of Gogol

Opposite the Winter Palace is the old General Staff Building and Ministry for Foreign Affairs; used for administrative purposes the two buildings together form a semicircle. Exactly midway between the two is a double triumphal arch. Both buildings were built between 1820–45 by Carlo Rossi. The triumphal arch was erected to commemorate victory over Napoleon's troops; as was the six-horsed victory chariot, by Vasily Demut-Malinovsky and Stepan Pimyenov, crowning the arch.

The former **Guard Corps Headquarters** ㉕ borders the east side of the square. The facade of this complex links the buildings by Rastrelli (Winter Palace) and Rossi (General Staff Building). At the end of October 1917 the defence corps followed Lenin's instructions to defend the city against the attack of General Krasnov's anti-revolutionary troops. A plaque commemorating this hangs in the south entrance.

To the west can be seen one side of the Admiralty overlooking the Senate's Square (*see pages 24–5*), as well as the **Aleksandrovsky Sad** (Alexander Garden, formerly Gorkovsky Sad), which runs parallel to Admiralty Prospekt. In the garden are busts of Gogol, Lermontov, Glinka and other personalities.

Where the Palace and Admiralty Embankments meet – between the east side of the Admiralty and the west facade of the Winter Palace – the Palace Bridge (Dvortsovy Most) joins the left Neva Embankment with the eastern tip of Vasilievsky Island.

In the middle of Palace Square stands the 47.5m (156ft) **Alexander Column** ㉖ (Aleksandrovskaya Kolonna). This monolith of pink granite was erected by the French architect Auguste Montferrand. Crowning the column is a gilded angel in the likeness of Alexander I. The column is taller than the Triumphal Arch in Paris's Place Vendôme, taller than Trajan's Column in Rome and taller than Pompey's Pillar in Alexandria.

Route 3

Nevsky Prospekt

In 1710 a path was cut through the trees in the southeastern section of the Neva Embankment. Transformed into a magnificent avenue, this path, first known as the Great Perspective Road, later took on the name of Nevsky Prospekt, after Alexander Nevsky (1220–63). Nevsky defeated the Swedes in 1240, and was later canonised by Peter the Great. His remains were transferred to the monastery situated at the end of Nevsky Prospekt, the Alexander Nevsky Lavra (*see page 50*).

Nevsky Prospekt

During the following century some of the period's most famous architects were responsible for creating the symmetrical shapes of the buildings. Between 25–60m (33–196ft) wide, the avenue stretches in a straight line for 2.5km (1½ miles) from the centre tower of the Admiralty (*see page 25*) to Znamenskaya Ploschad (formerly Vosstanya Ploschad or Uprising Square). From here, after a gentle right turn, it is another 2km (1 mile) to the Alexander Nevsky Monastery.

31

Along Nevsky Prospekt there are many museums, offices, companies, restaurants, theatres and cinemas. People come here to work, shop, sit in a café or just to wander around. Nevsky Prospekt is the equivalent to London's Oxford Street or Paris's Champs-Elysées. The most interesting section of this delightful avenue lies between the Admiralty and the Fontanka River. Almost every one of

Café sign in the Nevsky Prospekt

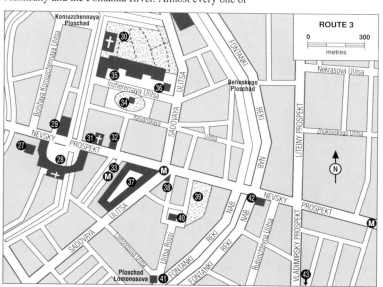

No 15 Nevsky Prospekt, one of the city's oldest houses

Traffic warden on Nevsky Prospect

these houses has experienced something of St Petersburg's history. All the buildings down to Znamenskaya Ploschad were built before 1917 except for the secondary school (No 14). At the beginning of the Prospekt, just behind the Admiralty, are the buildings that came into being at the turn of the century. These include, for example, the St Petersburg Trade Bank (Nos 7/9), or Palace of the Wollenberg bankers as it is often called, for which Peretyatkovitch used motives from the Venetian Renaissance (today it houses the Aeroflot office).

Outside the secondary school (No 14), the only new building (1939) in this section of Nevsky Prospekt, there is still a plaque dating from World War II bearing the message: 'Citizens! During artillery fire this side of the street is more dangerous.'

On the right-hand (ie south) side of Nevsky Prospekt, between Bolshaya Morskaya Ulitsa and Moika Embankment (Naberezhnaya Moiki), is one of the city's oldest houses at **No 15 ㉗**. It was built by Kokorinov in 1771 on the same spot occupied by the temporary wooden palace of Empress Yelisaveta Petrovna (Elisabeth I) from 1765–8.

On the other side of Nevsky Prospekt, No 18 used to be the Wulf and Béranger café, popular with St Petersburg's litterati. On 27 February 1837 Pushkin met his second here and then rode to his duel with D'Anthès, in which he was mortally wounded.

The land behind the Moika River on the left (ie north) side of the Prospekt used to be reserved for churches of a different faith, ie non-Orthodox. The first one is the former Dutch Church (Gollandskaya Tserkov, No 20), embellished with a shallow dome and projecting, Classical portico. Built in 1836, Jacquot modelled it on the tomb of Diocletian in Split in the former Yugoslavia.

On the other side of the road is a green building with white columns. It is the ★ **Stroganov Palace** (Stroganovevsky Dvorets) (1754, by Rastrelli), one of the most famous monuments to Russian baroque in this avenue. The sculptures at the main entrance, which represent sphinxes, were added at the end of the 18th century by the architect Voronikhin whilst he was restoring the palace. He had been Count Stroganov's servant during his youth and had lived in the palace. Today, part of the collection from the Russian Museum is housed here.

On the embankment next to the Stroganov Palace is the former **Razumovsky Palace** (Dvorets Razumovskogo), built by Kokorinov and De la Motte in 1766, and now the home of the Herzen the Pedagogical Institute (Naberezhnaya Moiki 48).

On the left-hand (north) side of Nevsky Prospekt take a look at the symmetrical form of architecture used for house Nos 22 and 24. Between them stands the former Lutheran **Church of St Peter**, built in Romanesque style (1838, by Bryullov). It now houses a swimming pool.

Nevsky Prospekt continues east to Kazan Square (Kazanskaya Ploschad), dominated by the ★★ **Kazan Cathedral** ㉓ (Kazansky Sobor, also known as the Cathedral of Our Lady of Kazan), the most beautiful edifice on Nevsky Prospekt. Designed by Voronikhin and modelled on St Peter's in Rome, the cathedral was built between 1801–11. It is surmounted by an enormous 90m-high (295ft) dome. For the construction of the cathedral cast-iron supports were used for the first time. The most distinguishing feature of the building is the magnificent semicircular colonnade, made up of 96 Corinthian columns hewn from Karelian Granite. The graceful effect of the exterior is mirrored by the 56 columns inside, which are crowned by bronze capitals.

The Kazan Cathedral

Standing in the niches of the porticoes overlooking Nevsky Prospekt are bronze statues of Prince Vladimir, Alexander Nevsky, St Andrew and St John the Baptist. Enormous biblical reliefs decorate both ends of the building. The cathedral is also a memorial to the victory won in the war of 1812. To the right of the entrance, it is possible to see the grave and bust of the old Field Marshal Kutuzov who, history records, collected himself here before leading the decisive battle of Smolensk.

Drawing among the columns of the Kazan Cathedral

By the beginning of the 20th century a kind of military museum had been installed in the cathedral to exhibit all the trophies captured from Napoleon's army after it was defeated in the snow of White Russia. There are also the keys to the 28 cities captured during the campaign, including Hamburg, Dresden, Leipzig, Reims and Utrecht. It is still possible to view these trophies.

Kazan Bridge and canal

From 1932 the cathedral housed the exhibition from the Museum of the History of Religion and Atheism, but it is now an active place of worship once more.

Opposite the cathedral at No 28 is the **House of the Book** ❷❾ (Dom Knigi). Constructed between 1902–4 by Suzor for the Singer Sewing Machine Company, the building, whose glass tower supports a huge globe, now houses the largest bookshop in the city and a series of publishing houses.

The House of the Book

Immediately behind Kazan Square flows the Ekaterinsky Canal. Cross the Kazan Bridge (Kazansky Most), built by Golenitsev Kutuzov (father of the great commander) in 1766 and considerably widened in 1805. To the left (ie north) of the bridge on the right-hand side of the Ekaterinsky Canal is the astoundingly beautiful ★★★ **Church of the Resurrection of Christ** ❸❿ (Khram Spasa na Krovi), also known as the Church of the Redeemer. Designed by Makarow and Parland the church was built between 1883–1907 on the spot where Alexander II was assassinated by members of the Narodnaya volya terrorist organisation (*see page 10*). The architecture contains elements reflecting the old Russian style – particularly reminiscent of Moscow's St Basil's Cathedral. However, Kiev's Vladimir Cathedral can be seen to have influenced the design of the dome. The famous paintings of the latter have been replaced here by mosaics.

The Church of the Resurrection of Christ

At the other side of the bridge on the left-hand side of Nevsky Prospekt, house No 30 is of interest. Concerts were held here by the Philharmonic Orchestra (founded in 1802), at which not only the best Russian musicians but also guest composers such as Berlioz, Wagner, Johann Strauss and Liszt took part. Today the Glinka Hall is used by St Petersburg's Philharmonic Orchestra.

At Nos 32/4 of Nevsky Prospekt stands the former **Catholic Church of St Catherine** ❸❶. Its facade reflects the transition from baroque to Classicism.

Farther along, on the corner of Nevsky Prospekt/ Mikhailovskaya Ulitsa and past the interesting Serebryanny Ryady (Silver Row) Building ❸❷ is the former **Town Hall** ❸❸ (Gorodskaya Duma) with its triple-tiered red tower. The town councillors in fact hold their meetings in what was originally planned as a concert hall. It was this tower that used to signal fires and floods; later it became one of the telegraph stations between the Winter Palace and the Summer Residence in Tsarskoye Selo.

Next to the old Town Hall an elegant Classical portico embellishes the end wall of the old Customs Gallery (1806, by Ruska). Today, it houses the city's theatre box office (teatralnaya kassa).

Opposite the Town Hall the short Mikhailovskaya Ulitsa turns off left from the Prospekt. It leads to the architectural ensemble of ★★ **Mikhailovskaya Ploschad** ㉞ (formerly Ploschad Iskusstv, the Square of the Arts). The design for the street and square was drawn up by the architect Carlo Rossi. The south side of the square is bordered on the left by the Grand Hotel Europe and on the right by what was, until the Revolution, the equivalent to the House of Lords (1834–9 by Jacquot). Today it is the main Shostakovitch Hall of the St Petersburg Philharmonic Orchestra; entrance Mikhailovskaya Ulitsa 2. Many top soloists have played here, as well as top conductors of the calibre of Karajan, Ferrero, etc. The St Petersburg Philharmonic Orchestra, which has performed in most of the major cities of Europe, is regarded as one of the best orchestras in the world. On 9 August 1942, during the difficult days of the blockade, Dmitri Shostakovitch's 7th (Leningrad) Symphony, which he composed in the besieged city, was performed for the first time in this concert hall.

Mikhailovskaya Ploschad

On the northern side of Mikhailovskaya Ploschad is bordered by the magnificent building of the former ★★ **Mikhail Palace** ㉟ (Mikhailovsky Dvorets), built by Rossi in Classical style between 1819–25 for the Grand Duke Mikhail, the younger brother of Alexander I and Nicholas I. The main facade of the palace is decorated with 20 pillars and a frieze consisting of 44 bas-reliefs. On both sides of the wide staircases are bronze lions. The wrought-iron railing separating the front courtyard from the square is one of the best examples of its kind in the city. After the Grand Duke's death his widow, the Grand Duchess Helene, turned the magnificent building into a meeting place for educated nobles and the greatest artists of the day. The musical soirées, organised by Anton Rubinstein, who engaged the best-known European interpreters, were famous. After the Grand Duchess' death in 1873 and then that of her daughter, the state bought back the palace.

35

Bronze lion outside the Mikhail Palace

The ★★★ **Russian Museum** (Russky Muzey, Wednesday to Monday 10am–6pm, closed Tuesday) was opened here in 1898, and substantial renovations were completed in time for the centennial celebrations. It is the world's largest museum of Russian art, containing more than 300,000 works from the fine arts, including paintings and sculptures. The collection ranges from medieval Russian icons to modern art. In the west wing of the museum, which overlooks the Ekaterinsky Canal, there are paintings from the Soviet Period.

The Russian Museum

Adjoining the east side of the building (Inzhenyernaya Ulitsa 4) is the **Russian Ethnological Museum** ㊱ (Muzei Etnografii Narodov Russii, Tuesday to Sunday 11am–6pm, closed Monday). This spacious museum comprises a series of rooms set out in parallel arrangement. Virtually every ethnic group of the old Soviet Empire is represented

Inside a Central Asian yurt in the Ethnography Museum

here – from the Baltic people to the Steppe people of Manchuria; from the Laplanders and tribes from the Polar region to nomadic tribes from the Moslem and Eastern population east of the Black Sea; from the White Russians to the inhabitants of remotest Siberia; from the Moldavians and Ukranians to the Armenians and beyond.

Reconstructions of house interiors and dioramas of native village life paint a clear picture of the great differences between the lifestyles of the ethnic groups. There are articles from Palech, Mstera and Khokhloma, toys from Vyatka and Vologda, embroidery, lace, carpets, inlay work from Georgia and Armenia, leather work, wood carvings, amber jewellery from the Baltic states as well as articles made out of bone from Lapland. The exhibits reveal the variety of the languages, cultures and civilisations.

The west side of the square is bordered by the house which was formerly the French Comedy Theatre, built by Bryullov in 1833 (facade by Rossi). Since 1918 it has been the home of the **Maly Theatre**, the city's main ballet and opera house after the venerable Mariinsky (*see page 53*). Next door (No 3) is the **Brodsky Museum**. Isaak Brodsky (1884–1939) was one of the best known painters of his day.

In a green enclosure in the middle of Mikhailovskaya Ploschad is a statue of Pushkin reciting his poetry, by the city's leading postwar sculptor, Anikushin (1957). Bordering Italyanskaya Ulitsa (formerly Ulitsa Rakova) on the southern-side of the square (No 13) is the **Theatre for Musical Comedies** (the so-called Blockade Theatre) and the **Kommisarzhevskaya Playhouse** (No 19), whose first production was staged on 18 October 1942.

Stretching over 280m (920ft) along Nevsky Prospekt from the Town Hall to the Sadovaya Ulitsa is the building of **Gostinny Dvor** ㊲, St Petersburg's largest department store (similar to GUM in Moscow). Measuring over 1km (½ mile) in circumference and housing 300-odd shops, this enormous two-storey building was once an inn (*gostinny dvor*) for travelling merchants, offering lodgings and a place to sell their wares.

On the opposite side of the Prospekt between houses Nos 40 and 42 (slightly set back from the street) is the light blue neoclassical building of the **Armenian Church** (1772, by Velten), which reopened in August 1993. A bit further on at No 48 is the **Passage**, a two-storey shopping arcade.

The Passage shopping arcade

Beyond Sadovaya Ulitsa, three houses further on at the junction of Nevsky Prospekt and Malaya Sadovaya Ulitsa, stands house No 56, erected in 1907 as the premises of the merchant Yeliseyev, and lavishly decorated in the art nouveau style by architect Baranovsky. Today it is one of the biggest food stores in St Petersburg, though it still retains its original elegance. On the top floor is St Petersburg's **Comedy Theatre**.

37

On the other side of the street (No 18) stands the ★ **Russian National Library** ㊳ (not open to the public). Founded in 1814, it is today the second largest library in the country, with over 20 million books. These include samples of Peter I's handwriting, the largest collection of incunabula in the world, and the 7,000-volume library Voltaire presented to Catherine II. The imposing building, which was built by Sokolov in 1794 to house a library, had to be extended by Rossi. The 18-columned main entrance borders one side of Aleksandrinskaya Ploschad. It was on the Prospekt opposite the library that government troops shot at the unarmed demonstrators on 4 July 1917.

The Russian National Library

Aleksandrinskaya Ploschad ㊴ opens out to the right of Nevsky Prospekt. The architectural unity of the square (1828) is one of Rossi's finest accomplishments. In a small garden in the middle of the square is a 4-m (13-ft) statue of the Empress Catherine II, surrounded by bronze figures portraying – in vivid likeness – some of the principal personalities who lived in Russia in the second half of the 18th-century, including Orlov, Potemkin, Derzhavin and Rumyantsev.

Behind the monument at the back of the square stands the **Pushkin Drama Theatre** ㊵, still known as the Alexandrinka. The theatre, designed by Carlo Rossi, was erected between 1828–32. On Nevsky Prospekt side of the building, an impressive colonnade consisting of six Corinthian columns adorns the theatre facade. The pediment is surmounted by the chariot of the leader of the Muses: Apollo.

The six Corinthian columns of the Pushkin Drama Theatre

Behind the theatre is ★★★ **Ulitsa Rossi** (Rossi Street), named after the architect, whom St Petersburg has to thank for so many of its magnificent buildings. This street is in itself a unique contribution to the design of the city. It is perfectly proportioned (220m/720ft long, 22m/72ft wide and with a building height of 22m/72 ft). The enormous windows of the facades, alternately paired off with semi-circular white columns, make it one of the most beautiful streets in St Petersburg.

The building on the corner of Ulitsa Rossi and Aleksandrinskaya Ploschad houses the Theatrical Museum, the Institute for Architecture and Town Planning and the Vaganova Ballet School, where famous dancers such as Pavlova, Nijinsky, and later Nureyev and Makarova trained. The **Theatrical Museum** (Teatralny Muzei, Wednesday to Monday 11am–6pm, closed Tuesday) records the history of Russian theatre and has a photo and record collection, which makes it possible to hear the voices of great singers and actors. The museum also owns the library of Marxist literary historian and theorist Anatoly Lunacharsky (to whom the museum is dedicated), as well as the works of Russian and foreign dramatists. In addition, there are manuscripts, models, drawings, sketches, and instructions concerning scenery.

Ulitsa Rossi leads into ★ **Ploschad Lomonosova** ⓬ (Lomonosov Square), another of Rossi's creations. In the centre of the square is a monument to Lomonosov (1892, by Sabello). Here the facade of the Bolshoi Drama Theatre stretches to the Fontanka Embankment. The house was built from 1831–3 by the architect Bryullov; the facade was Rossi's design.

Behind a beautiful wrought-iron railing on the eastern side of Aleksandrinskaya Ploschad, shaded by the trees

of a spacious garden, there is another fine example of Russian architecture, the **Anichkov Palace**, constructed between 1741–50 and frequently converted since then. The first main facade of the palace, commissioned by Empress Elisabeth for her favourite, Count Razumovsky, overlooked the Fontanka River, since at that time Nevsky Prospekt was not yet the main boulevard of the city. The main entrance was reached by boat. At the beginning of the 19th century, Quarenghi added the monumental building for the cabinet – the palace chancellery – which altered the view away from the river. Since 1937 the palace has been in the hands of the Soviet pioneers, and is today the House of Children's Creativity.

Behind the Anichkov Palace the **Anichkov Bridge** **42** (Anitchkovsky Most) crosses over the Fontanka. It is described as one of the most beautiful bridges in St Petersburg. In 1841 four bronze groups known as *The Horse Tamers* were set up on the bridge in pairs. In 1843 two of these sculptures were sent to Berlin as a present to the Prussian king; in 1846 two others were sent to the king of Nepal. In 1850 Klodt made new bronze casts to replace them and these can still be seen on the bridge today. Opposite the Anichkov Palace is another beautiful palace at No 41, built by Stakenschneider between 1846–8 for Prince Beloselsky-Belozersky.

The Anichkov Bridge

On the opposite embankment of the river (on the left-hand side of the Prospekt) is a further architectural monument (house No 34), the former Sheremetyev Palace (1755, by Chevakinsky and Argunov). The palace's semicircular parade ground is separated from the embankment by a cast-iron railing, bearing the gilded crest of the Sheremetyev family. Today the **Anna Akhmatova Museum**, which describes the life of the famous poetess who suffered so terribly under Stalin, is housed in one of the wings of the so-called 'Fontanny Dom'. When renovation work is complete, the palace rooms will be at the disposal of the Theatrical Museum.

Nevsky Prospekt then crosses the Liteiny Prospekt (leading off north to the Neva) and the Vladimirsky Prospekt (travelling south). The latter comes to an end in front of the **Vladimir Church** **43** on Vladimirskaya Ploschad, a magnificent monument to Russian architecture from the 18th century, with its impressive bell tower and five domes. Nearby, in Kuznechny Pereulok, is the lavish **Kuznechny vegetable market** (Tuesday to Sunday 9am–7pm, closed Monday).

The Vladimir Church

Finally, Nevsky Prospekt leads into Znamenskaya Ploshchad (for a detailed description *see Route 5*). On the right side of the square is Moscow Station (Moskovsky Vokzal). On the left is the metro station and the Oktyabrskaya Hotel.

Route 4

Palace Square – Field of Mars – Summer Garden – Engineers' Castle

The Winter Trench and the Atlantes of the New Hermitage

Lined by what were once manor houses, **Millionnaya Ulitsa** (Millionaire's Street – formerly Ulitsa Khalturina) is one of the oldest and most aristocratic streets in St Petersburg. From Palace Square it runs in a northeasterly direction. On the left is the New Hermitage (*see page 61*), its entrance adorned with 10 giant Atlantes designed by Terenenyev. Millionnaya Ulitsa cuts through the so-called **Winter Trench** (*Zimnaya Kanavka*), which links the Moika and Neva rivers and is crossed by three bridges. Of particular interest beyond the Winter Trench, at the far end of Millionnaya Ulitsa on the right at No 4 (corner of Apothecary Lane/Aptekarsky Pereulok), is the building that used to house the court apothecary, erected by Quarenghi between 1789–96.

Here, between the Dvortsovaya Naberezhnaya (Palace Embankment) and the Moika are many palaces formerly owned by court dignitaries. The **House of Scholars** ❹ (Dom Uchernikh) at No 26 Dvortsovaya Naberezhnaya was designed by Rezanov for Alexander II's son Vladimir, president of the Academy of Arts. Its impressive facade and the well-preserved interior, completed in various styles, are characteristic of Russian architecture from the second half of the 19th century.

Grand Duke Nikolai Mikhailovich's Palace (or former palace), north of Millionnaya Ulitsa at Dvortsovaya Naberezhnaya (No 18), was built by the architect Stakenschneider in rococo style in 1863. No 16 is the old English Club, so frequently mentioned in Tolstoy's *Anna Karenina*; No 14 once housed the similar New Club.

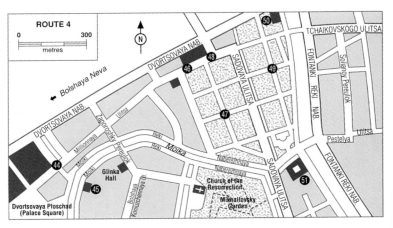

Not far from Millionnaya Ulitsa at Moika Embankment No 12 is the ★ **Alexander Pushkin Museum and Memorial Apartment** ⑮ (Wednesday to Monday, 10.40am–5pm, closed Tuesday and the last Friday of each month). It was here that Pushkin completed his novel: *The Captain's Daughter*; he also wrote the history of Peter the Great and composed the poem: *The Bronze Horseman*. After having been mortally wounded in a duel, the poet spent his last hours in this house. He died on 29 January 1837. Poets come to St Petersburg from all over the world to the traditional annual poets' reunion on the anniversary of Pushkin's death, where hundreds of poetry fans listen to their newest poems around the Pushkin memorial in the courtyard of this house.

In the Pushkin Museum

At the end of the Millionnaya Ulitsa on the left (house Nos 5/1) is the **Marble Palace** ⑯ (Wednesday to Sunday 10am–6pm, Monday 10am–5pm; closed Tuesday). Designed by Rinaldi between 1768–85, the building was commissioned by Catherine II for her favourite, Grigory Orlov. Orlov died before its completion and it later belonged to Grand Duke Konstantin Konstantinovich Romanov. Deriving its name from the granite and marble layers of its exterior, it is one of the finest monuments to early Russian Classicism. During the Soviet era it was home to the Lenin Central Museum; today it is part of the Russian Museum and home to its **Modern Art** department, which concentrates on modern Russian and some Western art from the early 20th century onwards and puts on some excellent temporary exhibitions.

41

On the right-hand side of Millionnaya Ulitsa are the old barracks of the Pavlov Guards. This vast building was erected between 1817–21 and designed by Stasov. In February 1917, soldiers from this regiment were among the first to join the insurgent masses. In October 1917 they took part in the storming of the Winter Palace. The main facade overlooks the ★ **Field of Mars** ⑰ (Marsovoye Polye) – a square that, in accordance with ancient Roman tradition, received this name because its main function was as a parade ground. Parades and troop inspections did indeed take place in the square.

Field of Mars

At the beginning of 1917 the Field of Mars provided the stage for mass demonstrations. After hundreds of workers and soldiers were killed or wounded during the February Revolution, the dead were subsequently buried in a mass grave in the middle of the square. Later the dead from the October Revolution, the civil war and a number of important people from the communist party were also laid to rest here beneath the flowerbed. In 1919 the monument commemorating the *Fighters for the Revolution* was unveiled. Many of the inscriptions on the gravestones were written by Anatoly Lunacharsky.

Lunacharsky, one of Lenin's active fighters in exile and a friend of Gorky, was the first minister for education under the new regime. It is thanks to him that countless treasures and artworks found in churches, castles and museums were saved from destruction. In 1957 an eternal flame was lit in the middle of the monument, from which the grave of the unknown soldier in Moscow was subsequently lit.

Leading onto this square in the north is the small ★ **Ploschad Suvorova** ㊽ (Suvorov Square), in the middle of which there is a statue to the Russian General Suvorov (1729–1800), one of the leading characters both in the Seven Year War and the war against Napoleon. The sculptor Kozlovsky has portrayed him as a Classical warrior.

Statue of General Suvorov

42

To the east of the monument, at the Palace Embankment 4, is the former **Count Saltykov Palace**, built in the Classical style by Quarenghi (1788). At the beginning of the 1830s, the owner of the Count Saltykov Palace, a daughter of Field Marshal Kutuzov, hosted roaring parties here, to which literary figures and politicians were invited. The facade of the building has remained as Quarenghi designed it in 1784; the interior of the building, however, was completely renovated in 1818. From 1863–1918 the building housed the British Embassy.

To the south of the Field of Mars it is possible to see the rear of the Russian Museum; to the east flows the Lebyashaya Kanavka (Swan Ditch Canal). Since 1715 it has linked the Moika to the Neva. Originally swans nested here, hence the name.

The Swan Ditch Canal

The canal divides the Field of Mars from the famous ★★ **Summer Garden** ㊾ (Letni Sad) to the east, popular with the people of St Petersburg looking for relaxation. The oldest garden in the city, the Summer Garden was laid out between 1704–12 on the initiative of Peter I by landscape gardeners Roosen and Surmin. The tsar spared no expense to make the garden as beautiful as possible. Most of the marble statues were designed by leading Italian masters. A total of 89 statues still line the avenues today. The *Peace and Plenty* monument deserves special attention. It was ordered by Peter I from the Venetian sculptor Baratto in 1722 and symbolises the Nystad Peace Treaty, signed with the defeated Swedes after the Great Northern War. Peter I also commissioned the statues *Architecture* and *Navigation*, an allegory representing the significance of the fleet and the development of St Petersburg. In the 18th century the statues of Alexander the Great, Julius Caeser, Nero and Claudius were also erected.

Peter the Great loved to make decisions for his subjects, even in their private affairs. In the same way that he would make political decisions, he would also make decisions

The Summer Garden

about the wearing of beards, the height of chimneys, the arrangement of parties, etc. On the one hand this resulted in stamping an absolutist seal on his reign, yet on the other it brought his country out of the Middle Ages and into the modern day with a western European flair. With the Summer Garden Peter I wanted to create his own Versailles. His court subjects were expected to attend the parties arranged here, together with their wives and daughters, whether it was convenient for them or not.

Today, the original arrangement of the park is only visible on old engravings. Between the canals, which were supposed to be reminiscent of Venice, stood rare trees and valuable statues, brought over from Italy. The conservatories, ponds, cages of rare birds, fountains, labyrinths and rare flowers were the pride of the tsar.

The park is no less beautiful today. The **marble statues** Peter the Great selected for the Summer Garden, moved around before World II, were put back exactly where the tsar had originally placed them. During the reign of Peter the Great only invited guests from the upper classes were allowed to visit the garden. Even after his death entrance was limited to small groups until the end of the 19th century. At the end of the 18th century its access to the River Neva was shut off by a cast-iron railing (designed by Velten and Yegorov). It is said that at the beginning of the 19th century the yacht of an English lord and patron sailed into the Neva and lowered anchor in front of the Summer Garden. The lord, known as an admirer of everything beautiful studied the railing from the deck of his ship for a few hours, without going ashore, and then ordered the crew to draw anchor. He explained that he had reached the goal of his trip. It would not be possible to surpass such beauty.

Statue in the Summer Garden

On the eastern side of the central avenue is a monument (1855 by Klodt) to the fabulist Ivan Krylov (1768–1844), whose works were translated into over 50 languages. Krylov, the Aesop of Russian literature, loved to go walking in this garden and often met with Pushkin here. Decorating the pedestal of his monument are reliefs depicting various animal characters from his fables.

The pedestal of the Krylov monument

On the Fontana Embankment, bordering the eastern side of the garden, is the ★★ **Summer Palace** ⑤⓪, built for Peter the Great by Trezzini. This was the first imperial palace in the new city, and is now open as a museum (Wednesday to Monday 10.30am–5pm, closed Tuesday).

Outside, the building is decorated with bas-reliefs glorifying the victories of the Russian fleet. Inside, each of the two floors of this modest, Dutch-style house has six rooms: Peter I lived on the ground floor and his wife Catherine I lived on the first floor. The interior furnishings of the palace, the wood carvings in the anteroom, the arrangement of the tsar's study and the empress's green cabinet, the tiled stove in the kitchen and lounge, the paintings on the ceilings, the tsar's wood-turning lathes, as well as many other personal items have all been preserved. Hence the palace's interior reveals a great deal about Peter the Great's character and his penchant for art and crafts. The interior looks like one of those bourgeois Amsterdam houses one sees in Vermeer's paintings. The faïence tiles of the big oven, a barometer from Amsterdam, as well as a heavy cupboard are all reminiscent of the Dutch town in which Peter the Great worked. The view over the canals with the cloud-covered skies and the large river nearby underline this impression.

Barometer in the Summer Palace

To the south of the palace there are two pavilions in the garden: the first, the **Coffee House** (Kofeyny Domik) came into being during the renovation of Peter's Grotto (Rossi), and the second, the **Tea House** (Chayny Domik) was designed by Charlemagne in 1827. The latter, a simple neoclassical pavilion, is now a gallery where it is possible to relax and drink a cup of coffee.

At the other side of the Moika – the southern border of the Summer Garden – is Sadovaya Ulitsa, which stretches to the Nevsky Prospekt. On the right is the Mikhailovsky Garden, designed with Rossi's participation in the 19th century. On the left is the **Engineers' Castle** ⑤①(Inzhenerny Zamok). It is worth taking a stroll round the outside of this castle, built for Tsar Paul I at the end of the 18th century, since the design of each side was made to match the surrounding countryside. Hence, for example, the north side overlooking the garden is more beautiful than the south side, which overlooking the parade ground and the changing of the guard, shouts strict ceremony. Since Paul I feared an assassination attempt and did not want to stay in the Winter Palace, he ordered his new residence to be made inaccessible. When it was built, the castle was surrounded by a moat. Drawbridges were lowered down over the canals from the man-made island, guarded by cannons. Nevertheless, none of these precautions managed to save Paul I. Forty days after he had moved into the castle (1801) he was – with the approval of his son, the future Tsar Alexander I – strangled in his bedroom by officers of his personal guard.

Afterwards, members of the imperial family began to avoid the castle. In 1822 it became the address of Russia's first Military Engineering School, which had been started by Peter I in 1712. Field Marshal Kutuzov later attended the school; in 1838 the 16-year-old Dostoyevsky was also sent here. It was while studying in the gloomy Engineers' Castle that he first started to write. When the adjoining land was redeveloped in 1958, this opened up a magnificent view of the south front of the palace, where a bronze statue of Peter I was erected in 1800. The model for the statue was prepared in 1715 (during Peter I's own lifetime) by Bartolomeo Carlo Rastrelli, the father of the famous architect. The pedestal is adorned with two bas-reliefs: *The Battle of Poltava* and *The Battle of Gangut*, as well as an allegorical composition of trophies.

The lane known as Maple Alley (Klenovaya Alleya), runs down what was Paul's parade ground in the 1820s; it is now an outdoor market for tourists. A little further south is the building which formerly housed the Mikhailovsky Riding School, built between 1788–1801 and renovated by Brenna and Rossi in 1824.

45

The Engineer's Castle

Route 5

The East End

Anichkov Bridge

From Nevsky Prospekt, east of the Anichkov Bridge (*see Route 3*), **Liteiny Prospekt**, one of the city's main arteries, leads out to the north. It is named after the foundry (Liteiny Dvor), established in 1711 not far from the Neva Embankment. During Peter I's reign cannons were cast there. The continuation of the Prospekt forms the Liteiny Bridge over the Neva.

On the north bank, east of the bridge, is Lenin Square (Ploschad Lenina) and the **Finland Station ㉒** (Finlandsky Vokzal), a modern concrete structure erected after World War II. In the station courtyard stands a gigantic bronze statue to Lenin designed in 1926 by Yevseyev, Schuko and Gelfreikh. It commemorates a landmark historical event: on the night of 3 April 1917 Lenin returned from exile abroad, having learned about Nicholas II's renunciation of the throne and the fall of the monarchy. From the turret of an armoured car bearing the inscription *Enemy of Capital* he made his famous speech to the tens of thousands of workers and soldiers who had flocked to see him.

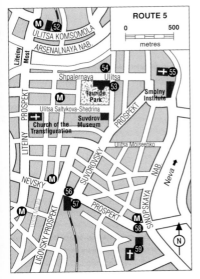

To the west of Liteiny Prospekt, the **Naberezhnaya Kutuzova** (Kutuzov Embankment) stretches along the south bank of the Neva. It was named after the field commander who also owned a house here (No 3). In 1812 he ordered the Russian troops to take up arms against Napoleon.

Running parallel to Naberezhnaya Kutuzova is **Shpalernaya Ulitsa** (Wallpaper Street). Until recently it bore the name of the worker Ivan Voinov, who sold the *Pravda* newspaper and was killed by the police on 26 July in 1917. There are many houses here that are of historical significance. In Furmanov Street which crosses Shpalernaya Ulitsa at the beginning (No 3) is Countess Yuryevskaya's former palace. She was the wife of Alexander II in a morganatic marriage. House No 18 is occupied by the Mayakovsky Club, St Petersburg's branch of the Writers' Association.

Farther east, Shpalernaya Ulitsa is bordered on the right-hand side by a relatively long line of columns and statues belonging to the former Barracks of the Imperial Guard (end of the 18th century), built in Classical style. On the ground floor the frontage is dominated by a powerful eight-columned Doric portico. Statues of the Ancient Roman god of war, Mars, and the goddess of war, Bellona, stand beside the portico.

On the same side of the street, a little farther on at Shpalernaya Ulitsa 47 is the **Tauride Palace ❸** (Tavrichesky Dvorets). It was built on the orders of Catherine II between 1783–9 for her favourite Gregory Potemkin, and designed by Ivan Starov. Potemkin's conquest of the Crimean peninsula (formerly called Tauris) earned him the title of Count of Tauride. Apparently, before the empress travelled into the deserted area of the Crimea, Potemkin had villages set up like scenery along the route in order to make it look like the area was flourishing.

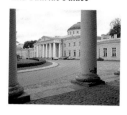

The Tauride Palace

The reserved, strictly classical lines of the palace's facade, with its use of ancient architectural motifs, contrasts sharply with its sumptuous interior. When it was built, the palace was one of the largest in Europe (65,700sq m/215,549sq ft). It had a considerable influence on Russian architecture and served as a model for many imitations.

Behind the palace a wonderful landscape park was laid out by Volkov, with ponds, canals, islands, grottos, an orangery and wooden pavilions in which lavish parties were held. Only part of the gardens remain today.

The Tauride Gardens

After Catherine II's death, her son Paul succeeded to the throne. He hated both his mother and her lover, Potemkin, so ordered the palace to be converted into a barracks and the 36-columned Catherine Ballroom to be used as horse stables. However, Paul did not reign for very long. His successor, Alexander I, ordered the palace to be restored to its original form; the palace has remained – since its renovation – unchanged to the present day.

From 1906–17 the imperial parliament sat here. In February 1917 the Petrograd Soviet of Workers and Soldiers' Deputies worked in the left wing of the palace, the Provisional Committee of Parliament, later to become the Provisional Government, in the right wing. After his return from 10 years of exile, it was in this palace that Lenin presented his April thesis, in which he sketched out the transition from a bourgeois to socialist revolution.

On the other side of the street, set back from the pavement, is one of the oldest houses in St Petersburg, the **Kikin Palace ❹** (Kikiny Palati), built in 1714. Its owners were executed because of their involvement in the conspiracy against Peter the Great. The building used to house the collection from the Kunstkamera. Later it was moved to a building on the Vasilievsky Island, specially erected for the purpose (*see page 20*).

The Smolny Cathedral

Shpalernaya Ulitsa ends at Ploschad Rastrelli on the east side of which is the ★★★ **Smolny Cathedral ❺**, one of the most significant historical monuments of St Petersburg. A number of buildings belong to the group, not all dating from the same period. The oldest complex, the Smolny Institute and the small collegiate Church of the Resurrection are located on land that used to belong to a tar house (Smolny Dvor). The site used to be used to boil the tar for Peter the Great's shipyards.

The Empress Elisabeth, daughter of Peter the Great, had a superb park laid out here. Between 1744 and 1760 Bartomeo Francesco Rastrelli, the master of Russian baroque, erected a convent for the empress, in which she planned to retire eventually. However, her wish was never fulfilled, since she died in 1761. Catherine II, who initially showed only a luke-warm interest in the work started under her predecessor, soon dismissed Rastrelli from her service.

The centre of Rastrelli's convent consists of the five-towered, opulent **Resurrection New Convent of the Virgin** (Voskresensky Novodevichy Monastyr), built between 1748–64. The middle tower is 85m (279ft) high. The magnificence of the facade's design – decorative, sculptured embellishments, many columns, and the richly ornamented trimmings on the windows – is characteristic of 18th-century baroque architecture. The interior of the church, not completed until 1835 by Stasov, reflects the spirit of Classicism. Rastrelli had nun's cells arranged in a square formation around the cathedral. The facade of this section, which overlooks the courtyard, was completed in the form of two-storey arcades.

A concert and exhibition hall has been opened in the collegiate church. In the evening concerts include old Russian church instrument and choir music. Art exhibitions, where the pictures are sold, are also held here. Visitors can enjoy a wonderful panorama of the city from the 63m (206ft) Zvonitsa (belltower).

To the left of the convent, Velten erected the entire ensemble of buildings belonging to the Alexander Institute; a school for the daughters of bourgeois families. To the right of the convent, at Ploschad Proletarskoy Diktarury 4, is the largest section of the Smolny buildings, the **Smolny Institute**. Intended for the education of girls of aristocratic birth, the institute was built by Quarenghi between 1806–8 in the large courtyard at the back, which, under Soviet rule, was changed into a beautiful flower garden with fountains. The building is known worldwide as the Smolny. In August 1917 the students studying at the institute had to leave and were integrated into other schools. The Smolny became the seat of St Petersburg's soviets, the centre of revolutionary events, seat of the head of operations directing the revolt in October. During the night of 25 October (7 November) Lenin came here from his last hiding place and took over command of the revolt. That same day he wrote the call: 'To the citizens of Russia', in which he let them know of the dismissal of the Provisional Government and the transfer of power to the revolutionary, military committee. On the same night, the second all-Russian Soviet Congress, meeting in

Lenin in front of the Smolny Institute

Smolny, passed the two decrees brought in by Lenin concerning Soviet power: the decree concerning peace, which was to introduce peace negotiations with all warring countries and the decree concerning the dispossession of all large landowners. At the same time the first Soviet Government was formed.

Lenin lived in the Smolny for 124 days before moving his government to Moscow on 10 March 1918. He lived with his wife in two rooms on the first floor.

In the avenue leading to the Smolny entrance the busts of Marx and Engels have faced each other since 1932. In front of the entrance itself stands the Lenin memorial, unveiled by Koslov in 1927. On its pedestal is written: 'Long live the dictatorship of the proletariat'. Today, St Petersburg's local council has its offices in the building.

Bust of Marx

From the Smolny, the Suvorov Prospekt leads south to **Znamenskaya Ploschad** 🔂 (formerly Ploschad Vosstanya or Uprising Square). This square is mainly of historical interest, due to its connection with one of the most decisive events of the Revolution. On 27 February 1917 the Cossacks in Pavlov's Guard's Regiment refused to shoot at the unarmed demonstrators who were crossing the square. The Petrograd guard joined together with the workers.

Until 1917 there was an equestrian statue of Alexander III in this square, whose very solid presence earned it the nickname of 'scarecrow'. After the October Revolution it was transferred to the Russian Museum (there is a small copy in the Alexander Nevsky monastery). In 1985 a stele was placed in the centre of the square in honour of the 'Hero City' of the then Leningrad.

The Znamenskaya Church (Znamenskaya Tserkov) which lent the square its original name, was pulled down to make way for the metro station, which opened in 1955. Over the station, rendered outside in granite and inside

Znamenskaya Metro Station

with red marble, is a large dome. The station is decorated with illustrations portraying the major episodes from the 1917 Revolution.

The **Moscow Railway Station** ❺❼ , one of St Petersburg's five train stations, has been in existence since the Moscow–St Petersburg line was opened with great pomp and ceremony on 1 November 1851.

Alexander Nevsky Square ❺❽ (Ploschad Aleksandra Nevskogo) marks the end of the Nevsky Prospekt.

It was just a bit farther along the Neva, near the spot where the Izhora flows into the river, that in 1240 Alexander Yaroslavovitch, Count of Novgorod – since then called Nevsky – won his great victory over the Swedes, who were commanded by Birger Jarl. In 1938, Sergei Eisenstein used the name of Alexander Nevsky, the man Russians regard as both a national saint and hero, as the title of his first talking film.

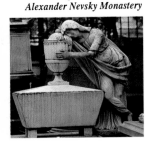

Sculptural detail in the Alexander Nevsky Monastery

As another memorial to Alexander Nevsky, Peter I commissioned the **Alexander Nevsky Monastery** in 1710, which later received the title of *Lavra* (Laura), acquiring certain privileges held by only three other monasteries in Old Russia: the Kiev Monastery of the Caves, the St Sergius Trinity Monastery in Zagorsk and the Potschayevsk Monastery in Volhynien. They were all the seat of an archbishop and all ran a seminary.

In 1824 the relics of Alexander Nevsky were transferred from Vladimir to the monastery. Just behind the monastery's main entrance, left of the main portal, is an 18th-century graveyard (formerly the Lazurus cemetery). This is the city's oldest cemetery, in which some of Russia's leading cultural figures lie buried.

The Trinity Cathedral

The centre of the monastery is the ★★ **Trinity Cathedral** ❺❾ (Troitsky Sobor), designed by Starov using earlier examples of Russian Classicism as a model and built between 1776–90. It is a tall building with a powerful dome, pushed together, so to speak, by its two belltowers. The main entrance of the cathedral is decorated with a six-columned portico, embellished by a sculptured gable.

Corinthian elements were used in the interior design. Brilliantly executed is the cathedral's iconostasis, for which Italian and Russian marble were used. Also outstanding is the gilded Tsar's Door.

Located in the grounds of the Alexander-Nevsky Monastery is the **Church of the Annunciation** (Blagoveshchenskaya Tserkov; 1722 by Trezzini) containing the **National Museum of City Sculpture** (daily 11am–6pm except Thursday), as well as the tomb of Suvorov, the great army general.

The best way to get to the monastery is to take the underground to Alexander-Nevsky Square (Ploschad Aleksandra Nevskogo).

Route 6

The West End

Along the Neva Embankment, west of Senate's Square, stretches the Angliskaya (English) Embankment (formerly Red Navy Embankment/Naberezhnaya Krasnogo Flota), so called because this was the centre of the British community. Most of the houses on the embankment date from the beginning of the 18th century. House No 4 is where the Decembrist, Truhetovsky lived. The first and second floor of the facade are decorated with 10 Ionic columns. Inside, the sparseness of the vestibule contrasts with the regal stone staircase which leads to the reading room. The Vorontsov-Dashkov mansion (No 10), built in 1738 and renovated in 1770, is a good example of how the facade of a rich villa was designed during the period of early Russian Classicism.

Interior of the Museum of the History of St Petersburg

51

Near the Nikolayevsky Bridge (formerly Leitenanta Shmidta Bridge) is the imposing ★★ **Museum of the History of St Petersburg** ⓺ (Muzei Istorii St Petersburga, Thursday to Tuesday 11am–6pm, closed Wednesday), with its massive 12-columned portico and sculptured frieze. The palace originally belonged to Nikolai, the son of Field Marshal Rumyantsev, who arranged for the house be turned into a public museum after his death (1826). The museum contained Rumyantsev's collected works of art, his library, Old Russian and Slavonic handwriting, as well as coin collections and medals. Since 1862 the bulk of the collection has been divided between various specialist museums and institutes (eg the library is now in Moscow's National Library). However, there are still some unique exhibits left: hand-drawn city plans and the original sketches of famous Russian architects, whose creations are visible in finished form throughout St Petersburg.

Section 1

The February and October revolutions of 1917: the first years after the October Revolution; Lenin's companions; documentary films; Gorky, Mayakovsky; artists and intellectuals who contributed in one way or another to the establishment of Soviet power. Models portraying the events of individual days in 1917. Photographs, posters and proclamations. The renewed reflation of the economy.

Section 2

Between the two world wars: the gradual expansion of the city; models, plans, photographs.

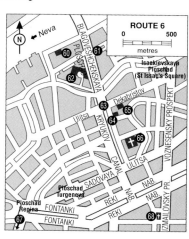

Section 3

World War II: the siege and front of the then Leningrad. This section is extremely well-equipped and presents the facts in a fair and unbiased fashion.

One room portrays a shelter, another the blockade of food supplies. It is estimated that at least 632,253 people died of starvation during this blockade.

Reconstruction of a home during the war; reconstruction of a home during the siege; the pressure of the war; the breakthrough in January 1944 after 900 days.

Section 4

After World War II: business life. Various branches of business in the city, of which shipbuilding, the clothing industry and the production of precision instruments are the most important.

On the embankment in front of the museum is an obelisk, reminding visitors that it was here that the *Aurora* was anchored (*see page 17*), the ship whose forward cannon fired the historic blank shot that signalled the storming of the Winter Palace.

Another imposing building on the English Embankment is the former English Church (No 56), in front of which are three statues. The room once used for prayer, which takes up the whole of the first floor, is decorated with Corinthian columns.

South of the Nikolayevsky Bridge is **Blagoveshchenskaya Ploschad ㊿** (formerly Truda Ploschad or Labour Square). One of the oldest buildings in the square is the **Labour Palace** (Dvorets Truda), formerly belonging to Grand Duke Nicholai Nikolayevitch, and now home to St Petersburg's local trade union committee. The palace was erected for Nicholas I's son between 1853–61 and

The Labour Palace

designed by Stakenschneider. The wealth of decorative embellishments make it a good example of 19th-century Russian architecture. The triangular-shaped island near the square, formed by the Moika, Kryukov and Admiralteysky Canal, is called **New Holland 62** (Novaya Gollandiya). It was here that the wood to be used in Peter the Great's shipyards was stacked. The Admiralty Yard and Galley Yard were linked by Galernaya Ulitsa (Galley Street), and by a few canals which, together with the Moika, formed a small island that served as a storage area. The old wooden sheds were soon replaced by brick buildings, and a beautiful granite arch was erected by De la Motte. During World War I there was a military radio station here. On 22 November (9 November according to the Gregorian calendar) 1917 this station transmitted Lenin's appeal for a cease-fire to all Russian soldiers and sailors on the front.

New Holland Island

South of Blagoveshchenskaya Ploschad, behind the bridge crossing the Moika, is Ulitsa Glinki. Not far from here, at 8 Pereulok Pirogova, the composer Glinka once lived. Here he composed his famous opera *Ivan Susanin (A life for the Tzar)* and *Ruslan and Ludmilla*.

Glinki Ulitsa runs into the expansive **Teatralnaya Ploschad 63** (Theatre Square). This is one of the cultural centres of St Petersburg, the city whose people show more appreciation for the theatre than anywhere else in Russia. Founded in 1730, the ★★**Mariinsky Theatre for Opera and Ballet 64** (formerly the Kirov Opera and Ballet Theatre) has seen such dancers as Anna Pavlova, Vasily Nijinsky and Galina Ulanova, as well as celebrated Russian composers including Katachurian and Prokofiev. The theatre is also the home of the Kirov Ballet Corps which has earned top international acclaim over the years and has retained its Soviet-era name.

53

The Mariinsky Theatre

During the blockade the theatre was bombarded on numerous occasions. By 1944 renovation work was complete and the doors were reopened with a performance of Glinka's opera *Ivan Susanin*.

Opposite the Mariinsky is the late 19th-century **Rimsky Korsakov Conservatory 65**, Russia's first university of music, designed by Nikol. Its students have included Tchaikovsky, Glazunov and Shostakovich. In front of the building are statues of Glinka and Rimsky-Korsakov.

South of Teatralnaya Ploschad, located in Nikolskaya Ploschad (St Nicholas Square) is the two-storey ★★**St Nicholas Cathedral 66** (Nikolsky Morskoy Sobor). Sometimes called the Sailor's Cathedral, it was designed in the mid-1700s by Chevakinsky, one of Rastrelli's pupils, in Russian baroque style with five domes. A magnificent row of columns, almost Classical in form, adorns the wall of the iconostasis. It is with good reason that these columns

St Nicholas Cathedral

are held up as an example of Russian decorative art during that period. The ★★iconostasis is carved in baroque style, gilded and painted. The cathedral's four-storey belltower stands in splendid isolation by the river.

South of Nikolskaya Ploschad, Sadovaya Ulitsa runs round the centre of town in a semicircle, ending at Ploschad Repina (Repin Square), named after the famous Russian realist painter who lived in house No 11 at the end of the 19th century. Repin painted many pictures in this house, including *The Zaporozhian Cossacks write a letter to the Turkish Sultan.*

About 2km (1 mile) south of Repin Square near the Obvodny Canal lies Narvskaya Ploschad (formerly Ploschad Stachek or Strike Square), scene of the first fatal clashes on 'Bloody Sunday' (9 January 1905), in which imperial troops opened fire on hundreds of peaceful demonstrators without warning (*Historical Highlights*). In the

The Narva Triumphal Arch

54

middle of the square is the **Narva Triumphal Arch** ❻❼ (Narvsky Triufalny Vorota), erected to commemorate the victory of the Russian army over Napoleon. The original arch was a wooden structure, hastily put together by Quarenghi to greet the victorious Russian army. This was later replaced by Stasov's brick version (1834), duly adorned with statues of great Russian commanders and a statue of Victory riding her six-horsed chariot.

From Narvskaya Ploschad, Ulitsa Pereskopskaya heads northwest to **Catherine Park**, originally laid out by Peter the Great for his second wife, Catherine I. (The palace that once stood here burnt to the ground in 1924.)

The metro station **Kirovsky Zavod** (Kirov Works) is layered with Caucasus marble. The station is dedicated to the workers of the former Putilov Works, the first raiding party of the revolution. The factory also played an important role during the blockade of the city from 1941–5. Production continued at the works, despite the constant bombing all around.

To the south of the Fontanka Embankment on Ismailovsky Prospekt is the huge ★ **Trinity Cathedral** ❻❽ (Troitsky Sobor), a local landmark with its five dark blue domes. Designed by Stasov between 1827–35, the cathedral is a fine example of Russian neoclassicism. It was here that, according to legend, Peter the Great married a young Livanian washerwoman named Katinka, better known as Empress Catherine I.

Trinity Cathedral

Just east of Trinity Cathedral, the **Vitebsk Station** was Russia's first train terminal when it opened in 1837. The existing building, dating from 1904, is an exhuberant Style Moderne construction with stained-glass windows and elaborately tiled halls. Also of interest from an architectural point of view is the **Warsaw Station** to the southest of the cathedral, built at the end of the 19th century.

Route 7

The Kirov Islands

This route passes through a fairly large area. Take the car or use the city's public transport facilities.

The islands in the Neva Delta, around which the Great (Bolshaya), Small (Malaya) and Middle (Srednyaya) Nevka Rivers flow, are known as Kamenny Ostrov (Stone Island), Yelaginsky Ostrov (Yelagin Island) and Krestovsky Ostrov (Krestovsky Island) or simply the Kirovsky Ostrova (Kirov Islands) for short. They once belonged to the nobility. On this land – bequeathed as ancestral estates by Peter the Great to his successors – great architects and landscape gardeners conjured up the country homes of the aristocracy.

The **Kirov Islands** were always a favourite place of relaxation for the people of St Petersburg, and after the Revolution they became a fashionable location in which to have a *dacha* (country house). A walk around the islands is an unforgettable experience at any time of year. There are a number of cafés, and lining the avenues are the palaces which used to belong to the nobility and are now used as sanatoriums and rest homes.

Yelagin Island

Krestovsky and Yelagin Islands

Even before World War II, **Krestovsky Island** had developed into the city's sports centre. The Dynamo and Iskra stadiums were opened, followed in 1950 by the **Kirov Stadium 69**. Sited on a man-made hill in the sea, it seats 100,000 and is the largest stadium in the country after the Lenin Stadium in Moscow. The Ring Terrace provides a superb panoramic view across the Gulf of Finland.

From the stadium Morskoy Prospekt, one of St Petersburg's most beautiful streets, runs east.

The Kirov Stadium

Paddling fun on Yelagin Island

The western half of the island, where the Kirov Stadium is located, is occupied by the **Primorsky (Seaside) Park of Victory 70**.

After World War II the population of St Petersburg answered an appeal to help lay the new park, and thousands of citizens joined forces one October Sunday in 1945. A total of 45,000 trees were planted. Today, the park covers a total area of 180 hectares (445 acres).

A bridge across the Middle Nevka links Krestovsky Island with **Yelagin Island**. Alexander I acquired the island in 1817 and made a gift of it to his mother, Empress Maria Fyodorovna. Architect Carlo Rossi and landscape gardener Joseph Busch were commissioned to remodel the island. The result was a large park with a series of man-made lakes and the magnificent, Classical **Yelagin Palace 70** (Yelaginsky Dvorets). Its interior, also designed by Rossi, was largely destroyed by fire during World War II, but the palace was restored a decade later using the old plans. Rossi's other creations on the palace estate are also worth seeing. They include the Orangerie, the kitchen wing and stables, the granite harbour and its pavilion as well as the music pavilion.

Until October 1917 Yelagin Island was the summer residence of the tsars, and the park – particularly the western tip – a place of diversion for St Petersburg's aristocracy. Magnificent parties were organised here. It was not until after the Revolution that the park was opened to the general public. In 1932 its name was changed to the Kirov Park of Culture and Relaxation. The entire island is planted with splendid trees and dotted with small pavilions. Facilities include a summer theatre , a vaudeville theatre, cinemas, restaurants, sports facilities, beaches and swimming pools. At the western point of the island, the so-called spit or **Strelka**, there is a ★★ terrace overlooking the Gulf of Finland. The views are superb, particularly at sunset.

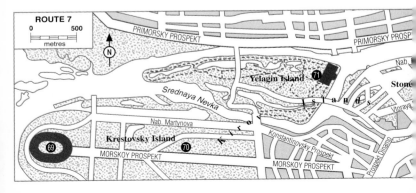

Stone Island and Apothecary Island

To the east of Yelagin Island is **Stone Island** (Kamenny Ostrov), until recently known as Worker's Island. From the mid-18th century it belonged to Chancellor Betushev Rumin, who had ponds and canals dug and the embankment fortified with granite slabs. Orangeries and hunting lodges were built here and bridges put over the canals.

During the civil war the first rest homes and sanatoriums were opened for workers in what had been the country estates of court aristocrats. These homes acted as a model for Lenin's 1920 decree ordering the creation of spa and rest homes of the same type throughout the country.

Of particular interest on the island is the ★ **Kamennoostrovsky Palace**  (Kamyennoostrovsky Dvorets), built by Velten for Paul I between 1776–81. The clear and simple lines of its exterior and interior design make the building an interesting example of Russian Classicism.

The well-preserved **Church of the Birth of John the Baptist** ⓭ (Tserkov Roshdestva Ioanna Predtechi) on the Kamyennoostrovsky Prospekt was built by Velten between 1776–8. Its pointed tower and lancet windows lend the building a distinctly Gothic appearance.

Church of St John the Baptist

57

As already mentioned, between the south embankment of the Small Nevka and the Karpovka River stretches the **Apothecary Island** (Aptekarskiy Ostrov), which is dissected from north to south by the Kamennoostrovsky Prospekt. To the east of the Prospekt, near the embankment of the Bolshaya Nevka is the **Television Tower** ⓭ built between 1960–3. It is 316m (1,037ft) high.

Covering an area of 16 hectares (40 acres) at the southeast end of the island is the **Botanical Garden** ⓮ (Botanichesky Sad, Wednesday, Saturday and Sunday 11am–5pm). The garden was first established in 1714 when Peter I planted an apothecary garden with all known medicinal herbs. It was this garden that gave the island its name.

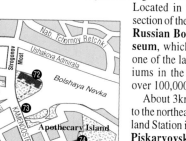

Located in the northern section of the garden is the **Russian Botanical Museum**, which looks after one of the largest herbariums in the world, with over 100,000 exhibits.

About 3km (1½ miles) to the northeast of the Finland Station is the famous **Piskaryovskoye Cemetery** where more than 500,000 victims of the Nazi Siege or *Blokada* lie buried in mass graves.

Lenin in Botanical Gardens

Route 8

Moskovsky Prospekt

The Institute of Technology

Plekhanov House

This route cannot be described as scenic per se, since the six-lane **Moskovsky Prospekt** – the longest avenue in the city – offers nothing really worth seeing apart from buildings dating from the Stalinist era. However, anybody driving to or from the airport, Pushkin or Pavlovsk has to use this road, hence its most important buildings deserve at least a mention.

The Prospekt begins at Sennaya Ploschad (Haymarket, formerly known as Ploschad Mira) in the city centre, crosses the Fontanka and Obvodny Canals, continues south in a dead-straight line past the Moskovsky Triumphal Arch and eventually becomes Highway 10, the main road to Moscow and Novgorod. It was on this road that Radischev left St Petersburg on the trip he describes in his book: *A trip from St Petersburg to Moscow.*

Founded in 1828, the **Institute of Technology 76** lies just south of the Fontanka Canal, at the intersection with Zagorodny Prospekt. It is considered one of the leading universities of the city. On the opposite side of Moskovsky Prospekt at No 19b is the Scientific Research Institute for Meteorology (Mendeleyev Institute). A monument to the great Russian scholar and what is purported to be the most precise clock in the world stand in the courtyard. Decorating one wall of the building is an enormous mosaic. It shows, in picture form, the periodic law of atomic weights formulated by Mendeleyev. Nearby, at No 28 is the vestibule of the Institute of Technology, decorated with 28 bronze medallions of Russian scholars, including Lomonosov, Mendeleyev and Pavlov.

On the corner of Moskovsky Prospekt/Krasnoarmeyskaya Ulitsa is the **Plekhanov House 77** built in 1800. The Free Economy Company used to have its headquarters in what was once the home of George Plekhanov (1856–1918), the 'father of Russian Marxism'. Lenin frequently visited the house, which was used as a secret meeting place. In 1905 St Petersburg's first soviets held meetings here for delegates elected by the workers. In a side wing of the building are Plekhanov's files and library, bequeathed by his widow to the history and science department of the Saltykov Shchedrin Library, of which this house is now a subsidiary.

Another example of fine architecture is house No 65 at the other side of the Obvodny Canal, the entrance to the former slaughterhouse (1825, by Charlemagne). Most of the buildings on Moskovsky Prospekt are not nearly as old. Particularly in the years immediately following the War, houses were built here for workers from the industrial areas. This green zone section of the Prospekt is 65m (213ft) wide. On the left in house No 98 is the **Pushnoy Auktsion**, where international fur auctions and exhibitions are held each January, July and October. Behind this building is the **New Convent of the Virgin** (Novodevichy Monastyr), where the poets Tutchev and Nekrasov are buried.

Commemorating the victory of the Russian army over Turkey (1828) is the **Moskovsky Triumphal Arch 78**. Twelve Doric columns made out of cast-iron form the imposing arch, designed by Stasov and erected between 1833–8. The height of the gate measures 25m (82ft). In the first half of the 19th century the arch was not just a triumphal arch, but also the gate to the city. Next to it stood a guard house, where travellers' papers were controlled. On the other side of the Triumphal Arch, the Moskovsky Prospekt reaches a width of 60m (196ft).

The main entrance to ★ **Moskovsky Park Pobedy 79** (Moscow Victory Park) is located opposite the nine-storey Rossiya Hotel. Like the Park of Victory on Krestovsky Island (*see Route 7*), this park was laid out by volunteer labour in 1945.

Flanking Heroes' Avenue, which runs straight through the park, are bronze busts of various noble citizens who fought for St Petersburg. The fountain at the head of the avenue shoots an 11m (36ft) jet of water. The 70 hectare (173 acre) park, with its man-made ponds and islands, is a favourite leisure spot for the local populace.

At the south end of the park, situated in Ulitsa Gasreilo, is the unique **Chesma Palace** (closed to the public). Built by Velten, this is where Catherine II would stay on her way to Tsarskoye Selo. Equally alluring is the red-and-white striped **Chesma Church** which stands behind the palace, built by the same architect.

To the east, at No 8 Gagarina Ulitsa (Gagarin Street) stands the modern, circular building of the largest sports and leisure complex in the city, the **SKK** (Sportivo Kontsertny Kompleks).

The Moskovsky Prospekt ends at **Victory Square 80** (Ploschad Pobedy), with a monument honouring the citizens who defended the city. Issuing from the central round tower are the roads to Novgorod and Moscow, the road to Pulkovo, Tsarkoye Selo (Pushkin), Pavlovsk and the airport and the road to Petrodvorets.

In the distance it is possible to see Pulkovo Hill, crowned by the largest observatory in Russia, the **Pulkovo Observatory** (the former Nicholas Observatory), built in 1839. During the siege, the observatory, including its optical instruments and library (the largest on astronomy in the world) was almost totally destroyed. But the establishment has since been renovated and expanded.

The Hermitage Museum

It is worth going to St Petersburg just to see the treasures housed in the world-famous Hermitage Museum in the Winter Palace, 34 Dvortsovaya Naberezhnaya (Palace Embankment). Open Tuesday to Saturday 10.30am–6pm, Sunday and holidays 10.30am–5pm; closed Monday.

Getting there: *Tram Nos 21, 26, 31; Trolley-bus Nos 1, 2, 5, 7, 9, 22 or Bus Nos 2, 6, 7, 10, 14, 30, 44, 45, 47, 60, 100. Nearest metro station: Nevsky Prospekt.*

Visiting time: At least half a day is necessary. A second visit is recommended to do the museum justice.

Tickets: The ticket desks are open until an hour before the museum closes and are in the foyer opposite the entrance. It is much more practical, however, to buy the tickets from the service office in your hotel, especially if you intend to visit the museum more than once.

Catalogue: There are no catalogues nor detailed plans of the galleries available, however there are places throughout the museum where it is possible to buy monographs, reproductions and slides.

The cafeteria and buffet are opposite one another in the Rastrelli Gallery, left of the entrance; this leads to the foot of the Ambassador Staircase.

Since 1946 The Hermitage Museum has occupied many buildings, linked one with the other, of which the largest is the Winter Palace.

The ★★★ **Winter Palace** *(Zimny Dvorets)* is the former imperial residence *(see Route 2)*. The **Small Hermitage** overlooks Palace Square. To satisfy her wish to add a palace to her own collection, Catherine II had the Small Hermitage built between 1764–75 by De la Motte, who was teaching architecture at the Academy of Art at the time. Shortly afterwards the empress united the Small Hermitage with the Winter Palace. In the Small Hermitage is the Pavilion Room and the Hanging Garden. The **Second** or **Old Hermitage** was erected on the Neva Embankment between 1771–87 by Velten, also for Catherine II's collections.

The **Hermitage Theatre** is separated from the main building by a canal. The bridge's shape is reminiscent of those in Venice and Amsterdam. Built by Quarenghi between 1783–7, the theatre is now the conference room of the museum.

Ten giant granite Atlantes support the portal (sculptor: Terebenyev) of the **New Hermitage** which is located on Millionnaya Ulitsa (Millionaire's Street). Nicholas I had the palace built by von Klenze and Strasser between 1839–52 as a museum open to the general public. It was opened with great ceremony in 1852.

Opposite: the Ambassador Staircase

Classical statue by the Ambassador staircase

The Winter Palace has only belonged to the Hermitage Museum since 1946. At the outbreak of World War II the treasures were taken to a secure place. The most important objects (1,118,000 in total) were stored in areas beyond the Urals and in Central Asia.

In 1995 a remarkable collection of 75 Impressionist and Post-Impressionist paintings taken from Germany during the war and believed lost was put on display. They remain on show though their future is uncertain.

Tour Guide: The tour described here virtually follows the route used by the official museum guide. Note that temporary exhibitions or restoration work can entail short-term changes to the rooms and items listed.

The various sections
The art collections housed in the Hermitage Museum are divided into seven different sections:
- **Western European art and culture**
- **Russian art and culture**
- **Antiquities of the former Soviet Union**
- **Antiquities of the Near and Middle East**
- **Classical antiquities**
- **Art and culture of the Middle and Far East (outside the former Soviet Union)**
- **Coin collection**

The Entrance Hall

After buying an entrance ticket turn left, cross the long columned gallery and go to the very wide ★★**Jordan Staircase**, made of Carrara marble and decorated with sculptures, gold plating and stucco. This architectural pièce de résistance was built by Rastrelli and restored after the fire in 1837 by Stasov.

Off the half-landing is the Field Marshal's Room (193) which goes through to rooms 200, 201, 202 (Gobelin Gallery) and 203, on the other side of which is the ★★**Pavilion Hall** (Room 204), a magnificent room with marble columns, gilded bronze balconies and 28 chandeliers, each one completely different from the other. Room 206 is the entrance to the Western Europe section, which starts in Room 207.

Floor mosaic in the Pavilion Hall

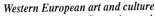

Western European art and culture
Occupying both the first and second floors, this is the richest section in the museum.

Italian art: 13th–16th century
207	Italian art from the 13th–15th century.
208	14th-century Italian art
209	Paintings from the second half of the 15th century.
210	Renaissance majolica and sculptures.
211	Embroidery

212 15th-century Italian art
213 Italian masterpieces of the Renaissance.
214 Two paintings by Leonardo da Vinci: *Benois Madonna* and *Madonna Litta*.
215 Paintings by friends and pupils of Leonardo da Vinci.
216 Mannerism.
217 Bartolomeo Vivarini, Boccaccio Boccaccino and Marco Basaiti.
218 Various paintings of the Holy Virgin with Child by various Italian artists.
219 Paintings by Titian and Pietro Marieschi.
220 Various Italian crafts from the beginning of the 16th century.
221 Titian Room.
222 Veronese Room.
224 Foyer with sales stand.
226 Italian art from the 16th century.
227 ★★ Raphael's Loggia.
229 Two masterpieces by Raphael: ★★ *The Holy Family* and ★★ *Madonna Conestabile.*
230 Michelangelo's unfinished sculpture *Young boy crouching*; majolica and bronze figures from the 16th century.

Titian

63

Italian art: 16th–18th century

231 Italian painting from the end of the 16th century and the beginning of the 17th century.
232 Caravaggio: *The lute-Players*. In addition works by Domenico Fetti, Orazio Borgianni, Pietro Francesco Mola and Bartolomeo Manfredi.
234 Neapolitan School.
235 Italian painting from the 18th century.
236 18th-century Venetian School.

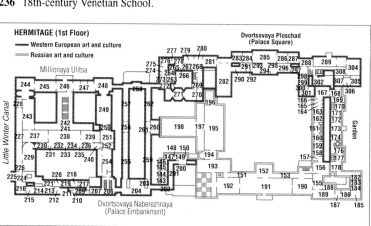

HERMITAGE (1st Floor)
— Western European art and culture
═ Russian art and culture
Dvortsovaya Ploschad (Palace Square)
Millionaya Ulitsa
Little Winter Canal
Garden
Dvortsovaya Naberezhnaya (Palace Embankment)

237–8 Large paintings from the 18th-century Italian School.

Spanish art: 16th–18th century

240 El Greco, Luis de Morales, Francisco Collantes, Rafaël Vergas, Francisco Ribalta.

239 Murillo, Antonio de Pereda, José de Ribéra, Francisco de Zurbarán.

At this stage of the tour it is worth looking at two rooms that show a different character to the rest. Go back through the two Spanish rooms and the last Italian room to:

241 History of ancient painting.

243 West European weapons and armaments from the 15th and 17th century.

244 Temporary exhibitions.

Dutch and Flemish art: 15th–18th century

245 Genre paintings.

246 ★★ Van Dyck Room.

247 ★★ Rubens Room.

248 Several works by Jan Breughel.

249 Tent Room. Early 17th-century Dutch paintings.

251–2 Genre painting, still lifes, portraits, landscapes.

254 ★★ Rembrandt Room.

Painting in the Van Dyck room

The Dutch collection

A staircase leads from Room 254 to the exit (room 206). Turn left at the far end of room 206 and go through room 204 to room 259, where the exhibitions from the Dutch School (north and south) begin.

German art: 15th–18th century

263–4 Religious works from the Gothic period.

265 German Renaissance paintings.

266 German paintings from the end of the 16th and beginning of the 17th century.

267 German paintings from the 17th century.

268 German paintings from the 18th century.

269–71 Western European porcelain from the 18th–20th century.

French art: 15th–20th century

272–4 Limoges porcelain and French paintings from the beginning of the 15th century.

275–8 French painting from the early 17th century.

279 ★★ Poussin Room.

280 Lorrain Room.

281 War paintings.

282 ★★ Alexander Hall of the Winter Palace, designed by Briullov in 1812. Contains collection of silver cutlery, for the most part French.

290–7 French arts and crafts. From here retrace your steps to room 283.
283 Portraits from the 17th century.
284 Watteau Room.
285 Boucher Room.
286 Portraits from the 18th century.
287 Chardin Room. In the middle of the room is the famous statue of Voltaire, by Houdon.
288 Greuze Room.
289 The so-called White Hall. Various portraits of Russian aristocracy.
304–6 Works from the 19th and 20th century. In 304, the Golden Salon, there is a ★★ collection of over 1000 cameos and combs by western European masters.

Room 306 adjoins Room 168, which is part of the Russian art and culture section (*see below*).

Watteau Room

French art: 19th–20th century (second floor)

332 Paintings from the early years of the 19th century. At first the tour does not visit the rooms in chronological order.
331 Two works by Eugene Delacroix as well as paintings by Ingres, Ary Scheffer, Delaroche, Charlet and Carle Vernet.

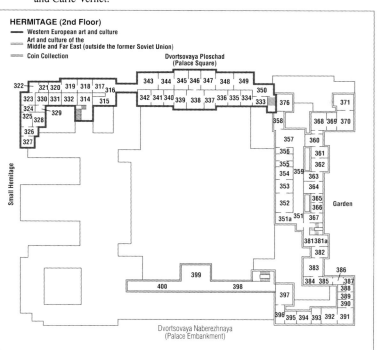

HERMITAGE (2nd Floor)
— Western European art and culture
= Art and culture of the Middle and Far East (outside the former Soviet Union)
= Coin Collection

The Matisse Collection

English art: 16th–19th century

The collection, arranged chronologically in centuries, includes rooms 298 to 302 on the first floor.

Russian art and culture (First Floor)

The regal ★★ Jordan staircase (*see page 62*) leads back to the first floor. Demanding the most attention in this section are the palatial rooms of the imperial residence. In addition to these rooms (190–198), are rooms 143 to 189, which are divided into four groups:

- Russia at the end of the 18th century and in the 19th century
- Russian antiquity and the Middle Ages from the 6th–15th century
- Russia under Moscow from the 15th–17th century
- Russia at the beginning of the 18th century

Peter the Great's Room

193 The Field Marshals' Room is named after all the marshals whose portraits decorate the walls.

194 ★★ Peter the Great's Room: This room was designed in 1833 by Montferrand and after the fire of 1837 restored by Stasov. The walls are lined with crimson velvet from Lyon and are strewn with Romanov eagles as is the high ceiling. At the back is the semi-circular exedra, containing

The Coats of Arms Room

the throne of Peter the Great, above it a large painting by Jacopo Amigoni (18th century): *The Tsar and Minerva.*

195 Coats of Arms Room contains the coats of arms of the different Russian provinces, as well as a permanent exhibition of Russian costumes. Receptions were once held in this room.

197 Gallery of the War of the Fatherland of 1812. In Rossi's room there are over 300 portraits of Russian generals from this period, painted by the Englishman G Dawe and the Russians Poljakov and Golike, as well as portraits of Alexander I and his ally Friedrich Wilhelm III of Prussia (both by the German Franz Krüger) and Franz I of Austria (by the Austrian Peter Krafft).

198 ★★ St George's Room, also Great Throne Room. Built by Quarenghi, this room is enormous (940 sq m/10,118sq ft). Its parquet flooring, whose bronze motif mirrors the ceiling, is made out of sixteen precious woods. The 48 columns made out of white Carrara marble are crowned with bronze capitals. At the back of the room, where the imperial throne is, underneath a bas-relief depicting St George killing the dragon (Francesco del Dero using designs by Stasov), there is a huge map of the former USSR. The map is a mosaic of semiprecious stones from the Urals: stars made out of rubies indicate the position of the most important cities of the former Soviet Union, whilst the names appear in emeralds.

Russian coats of arms **67**

St George's Room is connected to room 260, the last room showing the art of north and south Netherlands. Now return to the Field Marshals' Room (Room 193) and enter Room 192, the foyer of the Great Chambers.

191 ★★ Ballroom. This sumptuous room, the largest in the Winter Palace, is reserved for temporary exhibitions.

190 Concert hall. Here, in addition to the Russian silver pieces from the end of the 17th to the beginning of the 20th century is one of the biggest treasures of the museum; ★★ Alexander Nevsky's silver sarcophagus. Empress Elisabeth Petrovna had it made in 1752 out of the imperial coins minted from the first 1,474kg (3,250lbs) of silver mined in Kolyvan, Siberia. The richly ornamented tomb was intended for the remains of St Alexander Nevsky. Bas-reliefs show scenes from the life of the saint.

The Malachite Room

189 The Malachite Room: Bryullov's work (1839). The splendid green of the Ural malachite provides good company for the gold of the chandeliers and capitals. The last meeting of the Kerensky Government was held here during the night of the 7–8 November 1917.

188 The former Small Dining Room of the Winter Palace, in which members of the Provisional Government were arrested, has been preserved exactly as it was at that fateful hour.

155 The Machine Room: Peter the Great's personal collection of lathes.

The Rotund

156 The Rotund, a circular room with a coffered dome, contains an ivory chandelier, prepared on one of the lathes in Room 155 (a few details carved by the tsar himself); model of a victory column, which was to have been set up in a St Petersburg square; the uniform that Peter the Great wore during the Battle of Poltava.

157 The development of various craft industries.

158 Remarkable ★ bronze bust of Peter the Great (Rastrelli, 1723).

159 Room furnishings from the 18th century.

160 Wax life-size figure of Peter the Great (he was 2.04m/6ft 7in) by C Rastrelli, clothed in the royal gowns he wore in 1724 when Catherine I was crowned.

162 Portrait of Peter the Great by Lomonosov in the form of a mosaic.

164 Russian architecture from Rastrelli to Stasov.

165 17th-century portraits.

166 Russian porcelain; the first pieces produced by St Petersburg's imperial manufacturer.

167 Craft work from the 18th century.

169 Scientific instruments. The most important piece is the egg-shaped watch that belonged to Ivan Kulybin (1735–1818).

170 Portraits.
171 Decorative mural paintings, musical instruments.
172 Architecture (a continuation of Room 164).
173 Craft articles from the 18th century.
174 Large tapestry (1773). Gold-plated silver cutlery. Articles made from polished Tula steel: weapons, boxes, cabinets, chess games.
175 Furniture from the beginning of the 19th century.
176 Engravings from the 19th century with scenes from Russian life.
177 14 December 1825.
178 Book collection.
179 Small Pushkin room.
180 Room in 1830s' style.
181 Researchers and their discoveries.
182 Women's clothing from the middle of the 19th century. Embroidery and paintings.
183 Craft and folklore from the Ukraine.
184 First Empire embroidery and furnishings.
185 Craft from the middle of the 19th century.
186 Russian paintings from the 19th century.
151–3 Peter the Great gallery: these rooms are reserved for Russian art and culture from the period of Peter the Great (rooms 153 and 152) and of Moscow's rule (room 151).
152–3 Objects from Peter the Great's curiosity cabinet.
151 Russian art and culture during Moscow's rule in the 15th, 16th and 17th centuries.

Ornate door

69

The way to the exit leads through the seven last rooms of the Russian art and culture section (Russia from the 6th to the 15th century). Now go through the long gallery (rooms 200, 201 and 202), which houses wall tapestries from the 18th century as well as various Negro busts, completed in the exotic style of this period. Room 202 leads to room 143 and straight ahead to the Pavilion Room (204) and the foyer (206), where a staircase leads to the exit.

143 Slavic antiquities, 8th–10th century.
144 The country people of Old Russia.
146 Weapons and armour from the time of the Tatar invasion.
150 Crafts, icons, pieces of the old architecture, and articles used in daily life in Pskov and Novgorod.

Russian icon painting

Antiquities of the former Soviet Union
This section occupies the ground floor in the Winter Palace's east wing.

In the entrance hall, near the ticket desks, there are a few steps on the right side leading down to the lower rooms of the section.

Scythian relics

From the Palaeolithic period to the Iron Age

The collection occupies rooms 11–33 of the Winter Palace.

- **11** Palaeolithic to Mesolithic periods.
- **12–13** Neolithic period and Bronze Age.
- **14** Neolithic period, Bronze Age and the beginning of the Iron Age in Caucasia.
- **15–21** ★★ Scythian relics and artifacts. These are the most valuable exhibits in the museum and there are only copies behind the vitrines. The originals are in the treasury, rooms 122 to 126. To see these rooms it is necessary to have a special pass, issued by the museum authorities, and available through the service desk of some hotels or Intourist.

Altai culture: from the 5th–3rd century BC

- **22–3** Burial finds from the Kurgans of Tuekta.
- **26, 29, 30** Burial finds from the Kurgans of Baschadar.
- **24, 27, 33** The art and culture of the people who live in the southern Steppe.
- **32** The Yenisei area.

Art and culture of the people of Central Asia

- **34** Central Asia from the 4th century BC to the 4th century AD.
- **35–7** Central Asia from the 3rd to the 7th century AD.
- **37** Various Sogdian tools.
- **38–40** Central Asia from the 9th to the 12th century.
- **46–7** The golden horde.
- **48–9** Central Asia in the 14th and 15th centuries.
- **51–4** Central Asia from the end of the 18th century to the beginning of the 20th century.

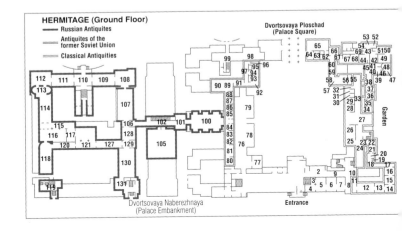

Art and culture of the peoples of Caucasia

Antiquities of the Near and Middle East

The collections from this section are on the ground floor.

Art and culture of Ancient Egypt

For the moment the exhibits are in rooms 81 to 91. (Entrance to the right of the Jordan Staircase.)

Ancient Egyptian hieroglyphs

71

Art and culture of Mesopotamia, Assyria and neighbouring areas

These collections are in rooms 92–6.

Art and culture of ancient towns on the Black Sea

On the other side of the rooms containing Greek and Roman antiquities is room 115.

Classical antiquities
Roman antiquities

The collections cover the period from the 7th century BC to the 4th century AD.

The Hall of Twenty Columns

Roman sculptures

Artifact from the Gobi Desert

Art and culture of the Middle and Far East (outside the former Soviet Union) (Second Floor)

Chinese Art

Mongolian art: 16th–19th century

Byzantine art

A silver salver

382 Boxes with ivory inlay (10th to 12th century).
★★Icons (12th to 14th century). Enamel works,
cameos, materials, ceramics, as well as coins and
medallions.

A triptych icon

Art of the Middle East

383–7, 391 and 394

The Hermitage owns the richest collection of
Sassanid silver dishes.

384 Craft articles made from bronze with copper and
silver inlays; vessel in the shape of an eagle
(8th–9th century); vessel in the shape of a cat
(12th century).

385–7 Iranian ceramics from the 12th to 15th century
with lustrous coating.

391–4 Iranian art from the 16th–18th century.

392 Miniatures.

388 Syria and Iraq, from the 13th–15th century.

389–90 Egypt from the 7th–15th century. A large collection of artifacts from the 7th–12th century.

395–7 Turkey from the 15th–18th century. Armour, hel-
mets, ceramics from Small Asia and Damascus.
Material, velvet, brocade, carpets, weapons.

Egyptian bas-relief

73

Indian art: 16th–20th century

The most interesting collections (rooms 368–71) con-
centrate on the reign of the Great Mongolian kingdom
of the 16th–19th century.

368 Marble, wood or bronze statuettes from various
provinces, Bengal, South India, Central India,
Gujarat, Punjab.

369–70 ★★Collection of Indian minatures from the 17th
and 18th century, belonging to various schools.
★★Collection of old Indian weapons.

371 Modern Indian art.

Japanese art: 17th–20th century

375 ★★Collection of wood carvings by the most important Japanese artists of the 18th century.

376 Modern Japanese crafts.

Coin collection (second floor)

Many thousands of antique, oriental, European and Russian coins belong to this extraordinarily rich collection. The
exhibits are displayed in the various rooms and galleries
of the Hermitage, according to their affiliation to this or
that culture.

Three rooms on the second floor, 398, 399 and 400, contain medals, insignia, decorations and various other individual pieces.

The Grand Palace at Peterhof

The Environs of St Petersburg

From St Petersburg, the following trips are to be recommended: Peterhof (29km/18 miles from St Petersburg on the southern shore of the Gulf of Finland; also accessible by hydrofoil), Oranienbaum (formerly Lomonosov, 11 km/7 miles west of Peterhof), Tsarskoye Selo (formerly Pushkin, 25km/16 miles from St Petersburg), Pavlovsk (27km/17 miles from St Petersburg) and Gatchino (45km/28 miles) from St Petersburg.

It is not possible to get a complete picture of St Petersburg without making a visit to at least one of these destinations, all well worth the trip (*see Map on page 7*).

Peterhof (Petrodvorets)

The Lower Park at Peterhof

This terraced, landscaped park (approximately 800 hectares/1,977 acres) descends to the sea. Scattered between the 142 waterfalls and fountains are small palaces and pavilions. This Russian Versailles was commissioned by Peter I and its centrepiece is the ★★★ **Grand Palace** (10am–5pm, closed Monday), located between the Upper and Lower Parks. Erected by Jean Baptiste Alexandre Leblond, the palace was completely remodelled in the middle of the 18th century by Bartolomeo Francesco Rastrelli. He added the two side wings and galleries, thus connecting the main building to the castle chapel in the east and the pavilion bearing the coat of arms in the west.

Before World War II the rooms, salons, galleries and wings were an extravagent show of splendour. During the War practically everything was devastated – renovation work has still not been finished, but completed sections include the 270m/886ft facade of the central section (early baroque), the roof, the domes, the cast-iron balcony railings and some of the most important rooms.

Inside the palace, in addition to exhibitions of decorative and applied art, there is also a collection of 368 portraits by Italian painters from the 18th century. The ★★**Grand Cascade** is particularly famous.

The Grand Cascade

The best views are from the terrace in front of the Great Palace. This masterpiece of landscape gardening consists of 37 gilded statues, 150 decorative sculptures, 29 bas-reliefs, two sets of steps leading up to the cascade, 64 fountains and a wonderful grotto. In the middle of a semicircular basin stands a gilded Samson, holding apart the jaws of a lion, out of which spurts a 20m (66ft) fountain. From the cascade a canal leads directly into the open sea. The tsar always used the sea route when he was travelling to Peterhof from St Petersburg.

The Lower Park forms a green backdrop to the Samson basin. The park was laid out in the 18th century and covers an area of 102.5 hectares (253 acres). Over 2,000 jets of water spurt from its 150 fountains. On the eastern side of the park is the Shakhmatnaya Gorka Cascade (1721, by Zemtsov), in front of which stand two powerful fountains – the Roman Fountains (1739 by Blank and Davydov; altered by Rastrelli at the end of the 18th century), which in their original form were reminiscent of the fountains in front of St Peter's Church in Rome. One of the avenues from the Roman Fountains leads to the huge Pyramid Fountain, so-named because its 505 jets of different heights form a pyramid of water.

A fountain in the Lower Park

Also of interest are the Sun Fountains and the series of Shutichi Fountains (from the word *shutka*, meaning joke), whose water effects are guaranteed to surprise visitors. The western section of the Lower Park uses the same plan as in the east, although it appears to be different thanks to the innovations of the architect.

Oranienbaum (Lomonosov)

The imposing palace of Peter the Great's favourite, Count Menshikov, is located opposite the Kronstadt Island fortress. On a hill facing the sea, it was built in the Russian baroque style between 1756–62 by Rinaldi. It was not until Catherine the Great's reign that the Chinese Palace was erected (1765). Dubbed 'Her Majesty's private *dacha*', the empress spent only 48 days here in the course of her 34-year reign.

Tsarskoye Selo (Pushkin)

The palace at Tsarskoye Selo was a present from Peter the Great to his wife Catherine II. Between 1719–23, the former country house was transformed into the magnificent ★★**Catherine Palace** (10am–5pm, closed Tuesday). Retained in its original rococo style, it is one of the most richly furnished palaces in the environs of St Petersburg and is without doubt one of Rastrelli's finest creations. It was completely destroyed during World War II and the restoration work is still being completed.

The Catherine Palace

The palace is surrounded by a park with monuments and sculptures by Italian masters. One wing housed the grammar school. Alexander Pushkin attended this school (for the privileged classes) from 1811–17. Today the school has become a subsidiary of the Pushkin Museum. To honour their past pupil the town of Tsarskoye Selo was renamed Pushkin but has now reverted to its original name.

Pavlovsk

The town is 2km (1 mile) southeast of Tsarskoye Selo. In 1777 Catherine II made a gift of the land on the banks of the River Slavyanka to her son, the future Tsar Paul I, in reward for the birth of as grandson who would continue the dynasty. After he ascended the throne, Paul began to decorate the two palace buildings and the Grand Palace, built here at the end of the 18th century. World-famous architects (Cameron, Brenna) worked on the palace and park, a project which was to become one of the most significant monuments to art by the turn of the 19th century.

Interior of the Grand Palace

The centrepiece of the ensemble is the ★★ **Grand Palace** (Bolshoy Dvorets; 10.30am–5pm, closed Friday). Today, there are 45 rooms open in the palace's museum, including the Italian and Greek rooms, the Carpet Cabinet, the War and Peace Room, the Throne Room, the Dining Room and the Portrait Gallery. In the palace there is an exhibition of Russian interiors from the 18th to 19th century. The 600-hectare (1,483 acres) park is laid out partly in French and partly in English style.

Gatchino

This town is located 45km (28 miles) south of St Petersburg. The palace park ensemble (10am–5pm, closed Monday) was begun in the mid-1760s. The architecture of the **Grand Palace** (Rinaldi, 1766–81, remodelled 1793–7 by Brenna), completed in the style of a hunting lodge, blends in perfectly with the surrounding countryside. In front of the impressive east facade are the **Upper and Lower Gardens**. Adjoining the palace walls is a small, pleasant garden, in which there is a statue of the goddess Flora, surrounded by marble satyrs and bacchants.

The many lakes, ponds and canals in the Gatchino park form a strange labyrinth. In the eastern section of the park on the shore of the Black Lake is the ★★ **Door Palace** (Privratsky Dvorets; 1799, by Lvov), unique owing to its technical design and reminiscent of a castle from the Middle Ages. Worth particular attention is the exterior of the palace which is interesting both from a technical and aesthetic point of view.

Opposite: interior of the Grand Palace at Pavlovsk

How the City Developed

St Petersburg at sunset

St Petersburg is recognised as one of the most beautiful cities in the world. However, it should not be forgotten that its magnificent buildings are also the visible expression of absolute power. Peter the Great used brute force to realise his dream of creating a city from the unhealthy Neva marshland. A demonstration of power and the repercussions of the tsar's traumatic childhood were decisive factors contributing towards the founding of St Petersburg. As a child Peter the Great had been eyewitness to gruesome massacres in the Kremlin; these left him with both a horror of Moscow and a nervous disorder.

Of course, there was a political motive for the founding of St Petersburg as well: the access that the city would provide to the Baltic, the window to the West. In order to achieve this goal, Peter the Great allied himself with the Danes and Poles against the Swedes, who then occupied the area around the Neva estuary.

At the beginning of the Great Northern War (1700–21) the Russians seized hold of the Swedish Fortress Noteborg, one of Novgorod's outposts during the Middle Ages. They renamed it Key Castle and settled down in the Neva Delta (*see Historical Highlights, pages 9–11*). The first defence was a very simple construction. On 16 May 1703 Peter the Great personally laid the foundation stone for the Peter and Paul Fortress on Hare Island (Zayachi Ostrov); this was followed in 1704 by the foundation stone for the Admiralty. In order to defend these buildings against attack from the sea, Kronstadt fortress was built on Kotlin Island. When his troops subsequently conquered King Charles XII of Sweden's hitherto invincible army, Peter the Great saw the victory as confirmation of the fact that he had made the right move.

Statue of Peter the Great

The tsar was the first European potentate to conceive and organise his city as an architectural whole. Having first dreamt of having the city modelled on Amsterdam, Peter the Great changed his mind during a trip to France, and chose the French architect Leblond to draft ground plans for the new city.

Creating one of the world's most beautiful cities from the deserted and rough woodland, involved hundreds of thousands of soldiers who were turned into bricklayers. Swedish prisoners-of-war, Finns and members of ethnic minorities were brought in as forced labourers; they drove stakes into the marshy ground and transported blocks of granite and stone to the site with their bare hands.

To populate the new residence (as of 1712) a *Ukaz* (decree) was issued commanding people from all over the Russian empire to move to the city. Due to the shortage of Masons, it was, for many years, forbidden to build in stone in any city other than St Petersburg. Every barge and ship importing goods to the city had to carry a certain amount of stone aboard, and every citizen owning more than 500 serfs was obliged to build a two-storey stone building in St Petersburg at his own expense. The town was often destroyed by flooding, but each time it was rebuilt, bigger and better than before.

The tsar did not just want to leave a shining example of architectural creation to posterity; his autocratic standards were such that he wanted to breathe intellectual life into his work too. St Petersburg was to become a centre of learning. With the help of Leibnitz, the German rationalist philosopher and mathematician, he worked on a project for the creation of a Science Academy and various institutes. It was planned that foreign professors would educate Russian students here, and at the same time young Russians would be sent abroad to study at universities in western Europe.

St Petersburg soon ranked with Paris and Rome as one of the most beautiful cities in the world. It was regarded as the complete work of an absolute ruler whose superhuman efforts had brought the Russian empire to the forefront of the international scene.

The reign of Elisabeth Petrovna, daughter of Peter the Great, saw the construction of the Winter Palace by Italian architect Bartolomo Rastrelli, the Smolny Cathedral and the enormous Tsarskoye Selo Palace, which until its almost total destruction during World War II, ranked as one of the most magnificent baroque buildings in Europe.

Winter Palace and (below) Winter Embankment

The grandeur of the city was augmented again by Catherine II, the wife of Peter III (nephew and heir to Elisabeth, who was deposed and murdered in 1762). During her reign the transition from baroque to Classicism began: Rinaldi created the Marble Palace, the Pavlovsk Palace was begun by Cameron, the Academy of Fine Arts was built by Vallin de la Motte, and Cameron made improvements to the Tsarskoye Selo Palace (to such an extent that it took on the proportions of a new building).

The window that Peter the Great had opened to western Europe, only to be virtually closed by Elisabeth, was flung wide open again by Catherine II. She was held by the intellectual elite of Europe to be a well-educated and committed ruler, an enlightened autocrat who conducted lengthy correspondences with Voltaire and other philosophers. At the same time, she had all those who tried to realise the ideas of these philosophers thrown into the dungeons of the Peter and Paul Fortress. Using architects, sculptors and well-diggers brought from France and Italy, the empress completely remodelled the Neva Islands; she had wide avenues and spacious parks laid out, large and small palaces built. During her reign the Winter Palace

The General Staff Building

Statue of Alexander Pushkin

was completed, the Small Hermitage was built, and construction of the second (Old) Hermitage was started (*see pages 29* and *61*).

Paul I, her successor to the throne, did not resemble his extraordinary mother in any way; apart from that he detested her. What he did for St Petersburg, he did for purely selfish reasons. He was neither concerned with Russia nor the size of the empire. His only concern was his personal well-being. It was for this reason that the Engineers' Castle was built (near the Summer Garden). He could have saved himself the expense though, since he was murdered there 40 days after moving in.

Alexander I's role as head of the coalition formed against Napoleon made St Petersburg Europe's diplomatic capital. During his reign the Italian architect Carlo Rossi built numerous yellow and white palaces including: the General Staff Building, the two pavilions of the Anichkov Palace, the palace on what is now Rossi Street and the one in Lomonosov Square, as well as the marvellous Mikhailovsky Square, bordered by the Mikhail Palace and other Rossi creations.

Although subsequent tsars continued to commission new buildings in St Petersburg, these were no longer as unified and accomplished as in the earlier years. The days of the well-balanced architectural ensemble were over. The tsars had other worries: the Decembrists' revolt was the first sign of the empire's vulnerability and Palace Square was now the arena for portentous events (*see Historical Highlights, pages 9–11*).

With all its architectural and courtly magnificence, St Petersburg was preordained to evolve into a cultural metropolis par excellence. In terms of having its praises sung, St Petersburg is probably the most literary city in the world. There scarcely exists a Russian writer, no matter where he was born or where he lived, who has not cherished St Petersburg.

Alexander Pushkin, the heart and soul of Russian literature, spent most of his time writing in the city; he loved 'Peter's creation' like nobody else and created an impressive poetic image of the place, which inspired whole chapters of his *Eugene Onegin* (1833). Nicolai Gogol also lived and worked in the city before going abroad, and it was here that he wrote his best works, including *The Government Inspector* (1836). Although born in Moscow, Fyodor Dostoyevsky wrote almost all his novels in St Petersburg, which he described as 'the most abstract and imaginary city'. His masterpiece, *Crime and Punishment* (1866), is set in St Petersburg's Haymarket district. Leo Tolstoy came to the city on short visits; the English Club is frequently mentioned in *Anna Karenina*.

Music and Theatre

St Petersburg also evolved into the musical centre of Russia, for it was here that Russian composers tended to create their masterpieces. They include Mikhail Glinka, the unchallenged founder of Russian classical music and author of such brillaint operas as *Ivan Susanin* and *Ruslan and Lydmilla*. The Russian Musical Society, which introduced regular concerts, was established in St Petersburg in 1859 on the initiative of the composer Anton Rubenstein. One of the first graduates of the conservatoire was Peter Tchaikovsky, the greatest of Russia's symphony and opera composers, author of such masterpieces as *The Queen of Spades*, the ballets *Swan Lake* and *The Sleeping Beauty*, and suites like *The Nutcracker*. Shostakovich lived in the city and many of his best works were written and premiered here. It was during the 900-day siege that he wrote his *Seventh (Leningrad) Symphony* which was performed at the height of the siege in 1942, the same year that he left. Other composers whose careers have been closely linked with St Petersburg are Igor Stravinsky and Sergei Prokofiev.

Musicians in Costume

The number and quality of St Petersburg's cultural institutions remain one of its major attractions, providing as they do enduring testimony to the artistic achievements of the past. Alongside institutions such as the Hermitage and the Russian Museum, there are the city's many large and grand theatres and auditoriums. The Mariinsky Theatre, which during much of the Communist era was known, rather mysteriously, as the Kirov State Academic Theatre of Opera and Ballet, has long enjoyed an international reputation. It was at the Mariinsky that Russian ballet came to flower and is still thriving; its resident company is frequently on tour abroad.

Below is a list of all the important theatre and concert venues in the city. Visitors should note that theatre performances usually begin at 7pm and concerts at 8pm. There are no admissions after a performance has started:

Mariinsky Theatre (the opera and ballet theatre), 1 Teatralnaya Ploschad; **Aleksandrinsky Theatre**, Aleksandrinskaya Ploschad 2; **The Maly** (small) **Opera Theatre**, Mikhailovskaya Ploschad 5; **The Gorky Drama Theatre**, 65 Fontanka Embankment; **The Comedy Theatre**, 56 Nevsky Prospekt; **The St Petersburg Philharmonic Orchestra, Bolshoi** (large) **Concert Hall**, Mikhailovskaya Ulitsa 2; **The Maly** (small) **Concert Hall**, 30 Nevsky Prospekt; **Bolshoi** (large) **Oktyabrsky Concert Hall**, 6 Ligovsky Prospekt; **SCC** (Sport and Concert Complex), 8 Ulitsa Gagarina; **The Conservatory Opera Studio**, 3 Teatralnaya Ploschad; **Circus**, Naberezhnaya reki Fontanki 3; **St Petersburg Music Hall**, 4 Park Lenina.

The Mariinsky Theatre

Food and Drink

Food

The Russians love hearty meals. For breakfast there is a choice of bread, coffee with milk, tea with lemon, cocoa, sour cream, yoghurt, milk pudding, soft-boiled eggs omelettes, hot sausages, *tefteli* (meat balls), butter and marmalade. The main meals consist of three or four courses. On offer for the first course are egg dishes, sliced meat or sausage, aspic (with meat, mushrooms or fish), cucumber, prawns, fish salads, brawn, various kinds of fish or black caviar. This is followed by soup. Popular from the selection available are: *schi* (cabbage soup), *borsch* (beetroot and meat soup with sour cream), *rassolnik* (kidney soup with gherkins), meat ball soup; summertime favourites include: *Botvinya* (cold soup with smoked fish, radish, beetroot and cucumber) or *akróshka* (cooked meat, smoked sausage, hard-boiled eggs, finely sliced onion and fresh cucumbers with kvas, served ice-cold).

Dinner is served

83

For the main dish there is a choice of beef and pork joints, chicken, duck, game, mushroom dishes, fish (eg salmon, sturgeon, pike-perch, sterlet) with potatoes, beets, cucumbers, vegetables, salad, and so on. For dessert there are cakes, biscuits, semolina or buckwheat *blinschiki* (pancakes) with sweet sauces, curd or apples, stewed fruit, *kisyel* (a dish which made from fruit juice or fresh berries, dried fruit and potato flour).

Russian cooking is enriched by the different regional specialities. From the Ukraine comes Chicken Kiev as well as *galushki* (pastry with a meat or curd cheese filling). Also to be found in St Petersburg are Georgian *shashlik*, Armenian-Turkish *dolma* dishes (minced meat in tomatoes, cucumbers, paprika etc), *chebureki* (meat pasties) from the Crimea and *pelmeni* (ravioli) from Siberia.

Drink

In the drink line, the big restaurants stock: tea, mineral water, fruit juices, beer, vodka, Georgian dry wines, Ukrainian dessert wines, Moldavian, Azerbaijani, Armenian and Georgian cognac, Crimean sparkling wine, etc. During the summer *kvas*, a light, fermented drink made out of dried black bread with yeast and raisins, is offered for sale on the street. World-famous of course is Russian vodka. There are various kinds to be recommended: *Stolichnaya, Zolotoye Koltso, Starorusskaya* and *Sibirskaya*. Soviet champagne is also excellent, if you can obtain the dry – but expensive – *Sukhoye* variety.

Bar in the Grand Hotel Europe

Restaurants

One of the best restaurants in town, serving both traditional Russian and European dishes, is the **Troika**, 27

Contented diners

Restaurant sign

Zagorodny Prospekt, tel: 315 8415, which is decorated in the style of an old Russian mansion. It offers a very good stage variety programme as does **Na Fontanke,** 77 Naberezhnaya Fontanki, tel: 310 2547, St Petersburg's first co-operative restaurant. If you are interested, it is a good idea to book in advance at the Intourist service office at the hotel. Also to be recommended are: **Demyanova Ukha** (Damian's fish shop, traditional Russian fish restaurant), 53 Kronversky Prospekt; **Austeria** in the Peter and Paul Fortress; **Nevsky,** 71 Nevsky Prospekt; **Sadko,** Mikhailovskaya Ulitsa 1–7 in the Grand Hotel Europe (Russian and European dishes); **St Petersburg,** Kanal Griboedova 5, and the Swedish-Russian joint venture restaurant **Nevsky Melodii,** Sverdlovskaya Naberezhnaya 62.

The **Café Idiot,** 82 Naberezhnaya Moiki, is an atmospheric basement café serving breakfast, lunch and dinner. In the cosy **Chaika** pub, Griboyedov Naberezhnaya 14, there is a wide choice of Western beers. Visitors should note that since the introduction of new currency regulations in 1994 there are no more so-called hard currency restaurants in Russia; in the restaurants of the **Astoria, Europa, St Petersburg** and **Pulkovskaya** hotels, as well as the **Troika,** foreigners can now pay only in roubles or by credit card.

There are many restaurants where it is possible to dine à la carte. However, the choice of dishes in these restaurants is limited. All restaurants – with the exception of a few hotel restaurants – close at 11pm or midnight.

There are also cafeterias in the large hotels, where it is possible to buy sandwiches, other small snacks, cakes, pastries as well as the normal choice of drinks.

Café in an old railway carriage at Warsaw Station

Shopping

The best-known souvenir from Russia is a Matroshka doll, the gaily-coloured wooden doll, which when opened is found to contain a series of dolls, each one smaller than the one before. Red, gold and black painted wooden spoons as well as the lacquered boxes and brooches are increasingly popular with visitors. Also in demand are wood carvings; china from the Lomonosov porcelain factory; tableware; gaily painted toys made of clay; embroidered, knitted and leather articles; records with Russian folk or classical music; fur hats; head scarves from Orenburg and Pavlov-Posad; and of course Russian caviar.

Matroshka dolls

Most of these souvenir items can be purchased in the shops of the **Grand Hotel Europe**, **Kareliya**, **St Petersburg**, **Pribaltiskaya** and **Sovyetskaya**.

Food Markets

There are 16 so-called collective markets where farmers sell fruit, vegetables and other food products from different regions in Russia. The biggest and best include: **Kuznechny**, Kuznetschny Pereulok 3; **Andreyevsky**, Vasilievsky Ostrov, 18 Bolshoi Prospekt; **Nekrasovskiy**, 52 Ulitsa Nekrasova; **Sytny**, Petrogradskaya Storona, 3/5 Sytninskaya Ploschad; **Oktyabrsky**, Moskovsky Prospekt 4b.

The Nekrasovskiy food market

Shops

Warehouses and department stores: **DLT**, Bolshaya Konyushennaya 21/3; **Gostiny Dvor**, Nevsky Prospekt 7/9; **Passage**, Nevsky Prospekt 48; **Univermag Petrovsky**, Ploschad Stachek 9; **Moskovsky Warehouse**, Moskovsky Prospekt 191; and **Dom Mod**, Petrogradskaya Storona, Kamenoostrovsky Prospekt 37.

Souvenirs: Nevsky Prospekt 51 (arts and crafts), Nevsky Prospekt 54 and 92; **Souvenir Market** at Klenovaya Alleya (Maple Alley).

Art market on the Nevsky Prospect

Records: **Melodiya**, Nevsky Prospekt 32.

Second-hand bookshops: **Antikvarno-Bukinisticheskaya Kniga**, Nevsky Prospekt 18.

New books: **Dom Knigi** (House of the Book), Nevsky Prospekt 28; **Mir**, Nevsky Prospekt 13; **Technicheskaya Kniga**, Liteiny Prospekt 57.

Jewellery: **Samosvety**, Mikhailovskaya Ulitsa 6; **Yakhont**, Bolshaya Morskaya Ulitsa 24; **Agat**, Sadovaya Ulitsa 47.

Behind the memorial to Catherine the Great in Ekaterinsky Square is an artists' colony, St Petersburg's equivalent to Paris's Montmartre. Like Paris it is possible to buy paintings here too.

Getting There

Opposite: arrivals and departures

By air

There are five weekly flights from London with British Airways and three weekly flights with Aeroflot. There are also four weekly flights from London with Scandinavian Airlines via Copenhagen and with Austrian Airlines via Vienna; Swissair fly three times a week from London via Zurich. Delta Airlines have daily direct flights from a number of US cities including New York, Atlanta and Cincinnati. Planes arrive at the Pulkovo Airport, which is 17km (10½ miles) from the city centre; a shuttle service is available. There is a regular Aeroflot service between Moscow and St Petersburg (almost every hour).

Train at Warsaw Station

By train

Trains coming in from western Europe arrive at Warsaw Station. The journey takes 33 hours from Berlin and 48 hours from Paris. The Finland Station caters for traffic from the north; trains from Helsinki arrive here (via Vyborg, the trip takes about 7 hours). Trains from Moscow arrive at the Moscow Station and the journey from Moscow to St Petersburg takes 7 to 8 hours.

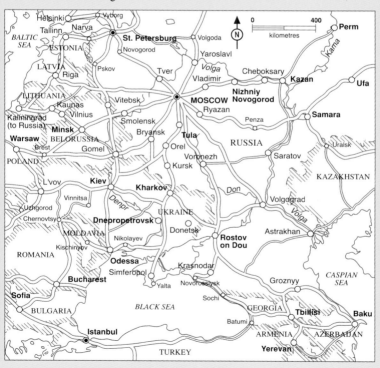

By boat

Cruise ship

All passenger vessels arrive in St Petersburg at the Sea-port Passenger Terminal, located at the southeastern tip of Vasilyevsky Island. Buying a cruise to St Petersburg might be a good idea since you do not need a visa, provided you spend every night on board your cruise ship.

Another option is to take a regular ferry boat to St Petersburg. Unfortunately, most ferry operations were halted in 1996 when the Baltic Shipping Company went into receivership. However, in 1997 a Swedish-Russian joint venture called Nordic Trucker Line introduced a new ferry service which connects St Petersburg with Ozelösund in Sweden. It is also possible to take the ferry from Travemünde in Germany to Helsinki, and onward either by ferry or by bus or train.

By car

Driving to St Petersburg has the advantage of making it easier to visit the beautiful surroundings of the city on the Neva as well as to obtain a better impression of part of the Russian country.

Driving from western Europe, the shortest route is from either Germany or the Czech Republic through Poland. From the Polish-Belorussian border at Brest one can proceed either via Minsk, Orsha and Vitebsk (in Belorussia), and on to Pskov and St Petersburg; or via Minsk, Smolensk and Moscow. St Petersburg can also be approached by car from Finland – the city is only 218km (136 miles) from the Finnish border.

Details of cars must be entered on the visa. *Carnets de passage* or *triptiks* are no longer required for private cars. Motorists who present their national driving licence at the border will be asked to complete a driving licence insert so that the information on the licence can be under-

Waiting for fuel

stood by the Russian authorities. Visitors who are intending to stay in Russia for longer than a month should obtain an international driving licence. All foreign cars must show a nationality plate. There is no obligatory Third Party Liability and the Green Card or international insurance certificate does not apply. Generally speaking, petrol cannot be bought for cash. Vouchers must be obtained at the border and from Intourist.

St Petersburg now boasts new service and repair stations for non-Russian cars. But you should still be cautious of the state of Russian roads. Diverting from the highways may get you into some unexpected adventures. Accommodation and petrol stations are few and far between. You may find that you are only allowed to stay at pre-booked hotels or campsites along your planned route. We recommend that you organise your journey through a recognised travel agency.

Further information can be obtained from Western automobile associations, Intourist and other specialist travel agencies (*see page 92*). Compared to Western countries traffic is very light.

Travelling within Russia
By train

As a traditional mode of transport, the railway, partly modernised with electricity and partly diesel, still plays an important role in national transport. Facilities in the normal trains are good, in the express trains excellent.

Passengers at a station

If you want to travel within Russia by train, there are transcontinental rail routes, such as those from Moscow to Vladivostok. They demand an adventurous spirit and a week spent in the train contemplating the endless Siberian landscapes. Food should be taken along since station buffet food is often not to the liking of weary travellers. Since train journeys are in great demand and the trains are often full, it is wise to book and pay for tickets at least two days before departure.

By air

Within the Russian Federation a busy flight network connects the most important cities. Inland there is only one flight class. Compared to the prices paid by western Europeans for the same distances at home, Russian flights are relatively cheap. Foreigners once had to pay for internal flights in convertible currencies, but since January 1994 payment for goods and services in Russia can only be made in roubles or by credit card. Apart from Moscow, there are direct flights from St Petersburg to Sotschi and Volgograd (Russia), Kiev, Kharkov, Odessa (Ukraine), Minsk (Belarus), Vilnius (Lithuania), Yerevan (Armenia), Tbilisi (Georgia) and other towns. Note that each state requires a separate visa, apart from Ukraine.

Getting Around St Petersburg

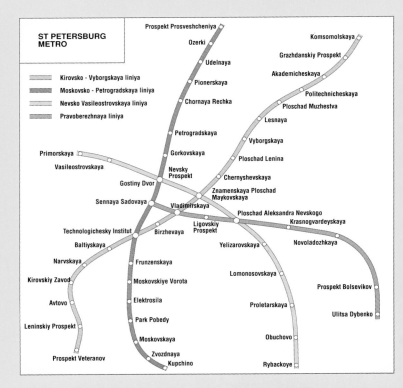

Taxi in Palace Square

Metro (underground)

The signs and underground maps with lighted routes make it possible to find the right direction quickly (*see map below*). The cost of a one-way ticket is subject to rapid inflation. Tokens are bought at the ticket office and these are fed into the automatic barriers. The Metro runs from 5.30am–12.30am.

Taxis

Taxis have a checkered strip along both sides of the car. The green light on the windscreen is on if the taxi is free. Today, many private car owners also provide a taxi service. Since most of these cars do not have a meter, it is best to negotiate the fare beforehand. Or you can order a taxi by phone (tel: 242 2022); 'West Taxis' are equipped with dollar meters (tel: 312 0022).

Hire cars

In St Petersburg and other large cities it is possible to hire cars without a driver (an international driving licence

ST PETERSBURG METRO

Kirovsko - Vyborgskaya liniya
Moskovsko - Petrogradskaya liniya
Nevsko Vasileostrovskaya liniya
Pravoberezhnaya liniya

Prospekt Prosvesheniya
Ozerki
Udelnaya
Pionerskaya
Chornaya Rechka
Petrogradskaya
Gorkovskaya
Nevsky Prospekt
Gostiny Dvor
Sennaya Sadovaya
Vladimirskaya
Ligovskiy Prospekt
Birzhevaya
Technologichesky Institut
Baltiyskaya
Narvskaya
Kirovskiy Zavod
Frunzenskaya
Avtovo
Moskovskiye Vorota
Leninskiy Prospekt
Elektrosila
Park Pobedy
Prospekt Veteranov
Moskovskaya
Zvozdnaya
Kupchino

Primorskaya
Vasileostrovskaya

Komsomolskaya
Grazhdanskiy Prospekt
Akademicheskaya
Politechnicheskaya
Ploschad Muzhestva
Lesnaya
Vyborgskaya
Ploschad Lenina
Chernyshevskaya
Znamenskaya Ploschad
Maykovskaya
Ploschad Aleksandra Nevskogo
Krasnogvardeyskaya
Novoladozhkaya
Yelizarovskaya
Lomonosovskaya
Proletarskaya
Prospekt Bolsevikov
Ulitsa Dybenko
Obuchovo
Rybackoye

is necessary). Further information about the different cars available and current hire charges can be obtained from the Intourist service offices in most hotels. Petrol and car-washing costs are the responsibility of the person hiring the car. It is also possible to hire a car with a local driver, and this can be arranged through the same channels. Avis are based at Pulkovo II airport, tel: 235 6444.

On patrol

Traffic police

Traffic police can be recognised by their white belts and shoulder straps. Their yellow cars are distinguishable by the blue horizontal strips and three large characters on the bodywork.

By trolley bus, tram and bus

The services run from 5.30am until midnight. Prices change just about every week.

A St Petersburg tram

By boat

From May to October it is possible to view the city from a steamer on the Neva (departure points: Senate's Square, Palace Square or the Embankment by the Summer Garden) or a river trip to Peterhof (departure point: Palace Embankment at the Hermitage).

91

On foot

Anyone lucky enough to be in St Petersburg for the White Nights should have a wander around one evening (nights when half the city's inhabitants seem to be on the street). Begin at Dvortsovaya Ploschad (Palace Square), walk along Millionnaya Ulitsa (Millionaire's Street) to Zimnyaya Kanavka (Winter Canal), then left to Dvortsovaya Naberezhnaya (Palace Embankment), along to Dvortsovy Most (Palace Bridge) and across the Neva to Birzhevaya Ploschad (Stock Exchange Square) on the Strelka spit. Thanks to the unique lighting of the White Nights the view from this spot, over one of the most beautiful parts of the city is doubly impressive.

Glossary

ulitsa street
bulvar boulevard
prospekt avenue
ploschad square
pereulok lane, small street
naberezhnaya embankment
ostrov island
storona district
dom house
most bridge
vokzal train station

Facts for the Visitor

A Russian visa

Selling tourist brochures

Travel documents

A visitor to Russia must have a valid passport and visa. The easiest way to obtain a visa is through a travel agent (*see below*). A tourist visa is valid for between 10 and 14 days, and varies in price depending on how quickly it is needed. On the visa are the date and place of arrival and departure as well as the length of the trip. Changes are only possible in conjunction with an Intourist office. It is only possible to extend a trip to St Petersburg after arrival. In order to obtain a visa the travel agency will require a valid passport, visa application form and one passport photograph. If you apply individually you will need confirmation of hotel reservations. Applications should be made at least one month before departure.

Customs

Antiques and manuscripts may not be exported. Items for personal use when travelling, such as personal computers, cameras, video cameras with film, tape recorders and portable musical instruments are permitted. Note that all precious metals such as wedding rings must be declared on arrival.

Exchange regulations

Foreign currency and other forms of currency such as travellers' cheques and letters of credit may be imported, but must be declared upon arrival on a customs declaration form. Currency taken out of the country must not exceed the amount shown on the import declaration. Importing and exporting Russian notes and coins is prohibited.

Travel agents

In the US:
Four Winds Travel, 175 Fifth Avenue, New York, NY 10010, tel: 212 777 7637; **Russian Travel Bureau** Inc, 245 E. 44th St, New York, NY 10017, tel: 212 986 1500.
In the UK:
Martin Randall Travel, 10 Barley Mow Passage, London W4 4PH, tel: 0181 742 3355; **Page & Moy Ltd**, 136–140 London Road, Leicester LE2 1EN, tel: 0116 252 4433; **Progressive Tours**, 12 Porchester Place, London W2 2BS, tel: 0171 262 1676; **Regent Holidays UK Ltd**, 15 John Street, Bristol BS1 2HR, tel: 0117 921 1711; **Scotts Tours**, 48A Goodge Street, London W1P 1FB, tel: 0171 580 4843; **Intourist Travel Ltd**, 219 Marsh Wall, Isle of Dogs, London El4 9FJ, tel: 0171 538 8600.
In St Petersburg:
Intourist St Petersburg Ltd, 11 Isaakiyevskaya Ploschad, tel: 812 315 5129

Intourist

Intourist, the former state travel agency, was privatised in 1993. Although it no longer has a monopoly on Russian travel, it continues to offer services in all the larger Russian cities and with its huge network of offices and agents, remains by far the largest travel company in the country. Intourist runs numerous hotels, motels, campsites and restaurants, organises sightseeing trips and conducted tours, and arranges the hire of cars, coaches and minibuses. Besides group tours, Intourist also arranges for individual journeys to Russia.

An Intourist bus

Currency and exchange

All major hotels have an official exchange counter, where you can buy roubles with hard currency cash, traveller's cheques and credit cards. In addition, there are *bureaux de change* throughout the city, many of which can be found in the larger shops. You will be asked to present your passport and visa.

Previously it was possible to pay in hard currency in the bars, restaurants and shops of the major hotels, as well as a number of other establishments including the special Beriozka shops. However, with the currency regulations that came into force in January 1994, it is now only possible to pay for goods and services in roubles and by credit card.

Russian roubles come in both banknotes and coins; kopecks are no longer in circulation. Details of current exchange rates are available from all *bureaux de change* and commercial banks.

The current fall of the rouble has caused rapid inflation and price instability.

Rouble notes

93

Tipping

The recommended amount is 5–10 percent of the invoiced amount. US$1 notes are always gratefully accepted, but watch out for waiters and waitresses who do not return your change.

Opening times

Offices: Monday to Friday 9am–6pm. *Food shops*: Monday to Saturday 8am–1pm and 2–9pm, Sunday 8am–1pm and 2–6pm. *Other shops*: Monday to Saturday 11am–2pm and 3–9pm.

Photography

Photographic equipment is easily obtained and there are quick film-developing services. Most hotels sell photographic equipment. Generally speaking, taking photographs in galleries, museums and exhibitions is permitted, though often at a hefty charge.

Making memories.

Public holidays in Russia

1 January (New Year's Day); 7 January (Epiphany); 8 March (Women's Day); 1 and 2 May (May Holiday); 9 May (VE Day); 12 June (Independence Day); 7 November (Revolution Day).

Festivals

Listening to rock music

In June every year the White Nights Festival runs in St Petersburg. During this period there is a full opera, ballet and concert (both classical and rock) programme with leading performers.

Post offices, telephones and telegrams

Main post office (Glavny Pochtant): Pochantskaya Ulitsa 9, (8am–10pm); every large hotel has a post office with facilities for basic postal services. Post offices usually open at 10am, but routine postal services are available at reception in the larger hotels between 8am–10pm.

Central telephone and telegraph office: Pochantskaya Ulitsa 9. Local calls may be made from hotels at no charge, but making an international call from a hotel can be expensive. There are public phone booths all over the city, and you can call abroad from many of them ('International'). The phones take phone cards which are available from post offices or Metro ticket offices. To make an international call, dial 8 + 10 + the international code of the country you are dialling (US 1; UK 44).

Time difference

St Petersburg time is three hours ahead of Greenwich Mean Time. In summer the clock is put forward an hour.

Electricity

The standard voltage in Russia is 220 AC. Sockets require continental adaptors.

Medical and other emergencies

In the event of illness or an accident out-patient treatment in the hospitals is free of charge. Medicine and hospital stays have to be paid for, although to start with it will only be necessary to settle for the hospital bed. The following hospital options are recommended:

AMC (American Medical Center), Serpuchovskaya Ulitsa 10, tel: 326 1730. Medical care to western standards, very expensive; **Poliklinik Nr 2**, Moskovsky Prospekt 22, tel: 316 5904. Well-equipped clinic with Accident and Emergency department.

Lost property

Sacharievskaya Ulitsa 19, tel: 278 3690; Vasilievsky Ostrov, 70 Sredny Prospekt, tel: 213 0039.

Accommodation

Hotels

The choice of hotels in St Petersburg is still very limited, particularly in the moderate price range. An individual traveller should expect to pay between £60 and £120 per night for a single room.

Expensive

Astoria, Bolshaya Morskaya 39, tel: 210 5757. Renovations in 1991 returned this fine hotel to its former glory; **Grand Hotel Europe**, Mikhailovskaya Ulitsa 1/7, tel: 329 6001. Situated on the corner of Nevsky Prospekt, this is the oldest hotel in the city, retaining much of its original art nouveau décor and furnishings; **Nevsky Palace Hotel**, Nevsky Prospekt 57, tel: 275 2001. Opened in 1993, this conforms to a good 4-star international hotel.

Moderate

Pribaltiskaya, Korablestroiteley Ulitsa 14, tel: 356 0001. Situated right on the Gulf of Finland, good rooms; **Helen**, Lermontovsky Prospekt 43/1, tel: 259 2048. A Russian-Finnish joint-venture hotel; **Ochtinskaya**, Bolshoi Ochtinsky Prospekt 4, tel: 227 4438. On the bank of the Neva, nice rooms; **St Petersburg**, Vyborgskaya Naberezhnaya 5/2, tel: 542 9411. Fine views over the city compensate for lack of comfort; **Hotel Ship Peterhof**, Pier Makarov, tel: 325 8888. A floating alternative.

Floating hotel

Youth hostel

St Petersburg International Hostel, Sovietskaya Ulitsa 28, tel: 277 0569. A good option for budget travellers.

Astoria Hotel

Index